Sandi's Anchor of Hope

a true story by

Romaine Stauffer

CHRISTIAN LIGHT PUBLICATIONS, INC.
Harrisonburg, Virginia 22801-1212

Christian Light Publications, Inc., Harrisonburg, Virginia 22801
© 1997 by Christian Light Publications, Inc.
All rights reserved. Published 1997
Printed in the United States of America

06 05 04 03 02 01 00 99 98 97   5 4 3 2

Cover by David W. Miller

ISBN 0-87813-568-5

Lovingly dedicated to my daughter,
Cheryl (Stauffer) Miller,
through whom I met Sandi
and heard her story.

We . . . have a strong consolation,
who have fled for refuge to lay hold
upon the hope set before us:
Which hope we have
as an anchor of the soul,
both sure and steadfast.
Hebrews 6:18b,19a.

Introduction

The number of abused children in our world today is increasing rapidly as society spirals downward. The rising divorce rate in North America is producing an unprecedented number of one-parent families. The innocent victims of these broken homes are the ones who suffer most. Statistics show that children from broken homes, or with abusive parents, often repeat the pattern in their own homes. They have not been trained to cope with the stress of normal living.

Tragically, these problems are encroaching upon the nominal Christian church. What was once unheard of is becoming more and more commonplace as churches accommodate, make excuses for, or rename sin. This paints a dark picture for society at large and for individuals caught in situations not of their own making.

Perhaps you are one of those trapped in what seems like a hopeless situation. Is there an answer? Is there any hope? This book is the personal testimony of one who found the answer and a way out of a seemingly hopeless situation.

Whatever difficulty you are in, or whatever your problem may be, there is an answer and a way out. You can find it in the same place Sandi did, for "seek, and ye shall find" is more than a nice cliché; it is a promise given by Jesus Christ to anyone in need.

This is the true story of a real person. Sandi does not want to draw any attention to herself, but to point the reader to the One who can meet every need and solve every problem. For this reason, and to protect the privacy of this story's characters, the names of all persons and locations have been changed.

My deepest gratitude, first of all, to GOD who is the Main Character in this story; for it is He who so marvelously led and worked out all the details. Special thanks, also, to Sandi and Philip for having the courage to expose their lives in sharing their story. I owe much to Leroy, my long-suffering husband, and to the three of my sons still living at home. They uncomplainingly allowed me to write when I could have been using my time to make their lives more comfortable.

Special thanks also to all those who helped critique my writing and refine it into the finished product.

To God be the glory,
Great things HE hath done!

—Romaine Stauffer

Chapter 1

The early morning sun streamed through the window above the crib, waking Sandi. Getting no answer to repeated calls for her mother, she sat down to consider things in her baby way. She barely remembered living anywhere other than in this little cottage with her parents in Roseville, California. The trip from Oklahoma to the Golden State was only a vague memory. She considered only two facts: she was hungry, and she was imprisoned in the crib.

Wailing, Sandi lay down and kicked her little bare feet at the confining bars of the crib. One of the bars suddenly popped out of place and fell into the crib, striking her on the head. Shocked into silence, she lay looking through the hole. Instinctively, she realized a way of escape had been made for her.

Sandi wriggled backwards through the gap and landed with both feet on the floor. Knowing from past experience she could not reach the doorknob without standing on something, she pushed the crib over to the door, crawled back inside, and

1

unlocked the door. Once more she wriggled out of the crib, pushed it back out of the way, and opened the door.

Sandi padded silently through the living room to the front door. After pushing a chair against it, she could reach the lock. Clad only in a diaper, she walked through the open door and crossed the gravel to the cottage next door.

"Mama, Mama," Sandi's little voice piped through the early stillness as she banged on the door, calling her aunt.

The door opened suddenly, framing an astonished Aunt Carmen.

"Sandi! What in the world are you doing here?" she exclaimed.

"I want brek-stast, Mama," Sandi explained simply.

Aunt Carmen scooped up the nearly naked two-year-old and stepped back into her cottage. Grabbing her own son, Robbie, by the hand, she marched back outside and across the gravel to the cottage from which Sandi had come.

"Karin," Aunt Carmen called loudly, knocking on the door of her twin sister's bedroom. "Come out here and see what I found on my doorstep."

Yawning and throwing on a torn housecoat, Sandi's mother appeared from the bedroom.

"What's the idea, getting me out at this hour?" she groaned.

"Your daughter didn't think it was too early to

get up," Aunt Carmen shot back. "I found her outside my door calling me."

"How did she get there?" Mama asked, amazed and suddenly awake. "She was in her crib and the door of her room was locked."

The crib by the door and the missing bar explained Sandi's extraordinary escape.

"She must have made an awful lot of noise," Aunt Carmen observed. "I don't see how you could have slept through all that. You must have been stoned."

"Oh, I was not," Mama protested. "I declare, that child acts more like her father all the time. She can get into more trouble. . . . Did you have coffee yet?"

"Yes, but I can always drink another cup if you're going to make some," Aunt Carmen said, sitting down at the kitchen table. "Just be glad she came to my door, or who knows where she might be wandering around in this town—and wearing only a diaper! Even if this is California, it's the middle of winter."

Mama reached for her cigarettes as soon as the coffee pot was plugged in. Taking some clean clothes from the pile on a chair, she sat down across from her sister and pulled a shirt over her vagrant daughter's head.

"Did Ralph find a job yesterday?" Mama asked the daily question.

"No," Aunt Carmen sighed. "Did Norman?"

3

"No," Mama echoed the answer and the sigh. "I wonder where all these wonderful opportunities are you claimed would be here. You and Ralph dragged us out here where there's supposed to be so much money, but I haven't seen any of it yet. I'm getting sick of it."

"You came of your own free will. We didn't make you come," Aunt Carmen disagreed.

"Yeah, but it was your idea in the first place," Mama returned. "You were there trying to talk me into coming out here when the trailer caught fire. Remember?"

"How could I forget?" Aunt Carmen replied. "The heater was making that popping sound, and the men said they'd check it when they came back. All of a sudden, fire was everywhere. You only had time to run back to the bedroom for Sandi and jump out the back door. I was never so scared in my life!"

"And all we could do was stand there and watch it burn to the ground," Mama mourned. "All Sandi's baby pictures . . . everything was lost."

"So after that, you decided you might as well come to California with us," Aunt Carmen reminded her twin.

"Well, it did seem like the thing to do since we had lost everything we had at home," Mama admitted. "But it isn't working out the way we had hoped. We're thinking of going back home again if something doesn't turn up soon."

4

A loud bang and a screech from the living room interrupted the sisters' conversation. They rushed out to find Sandi sitting innocently on the sofa above Robbie.

"Sandi push me down," Robbie wailed. Blood dripped from his mouth where he had bitten his lip.

"I guess she didn't mean to," Aunt Carmen soothed, heading for the bathroom to get a wet washcloth.

"I wouldn't bet on it," Mama muttered grimly, grabbing Sandi and giving her a whack with the back of her hand. "Didn't I say this child is getting more like her father every day? She is so strong-willed and stubborn I hardly know what to do with her. She's going to get herself into all kinds of trouble, just like Norman always did.

"I'm getting sick of him," Mama launched into her list of complaints about her husband. "I thought I'd be living on easy street when I married him. He always had plenty of money to throw around. What a joke! His parents had all the money; he never has any. Any money he gets goes into gambling and partying. Other women see more of his money than I do. If he doesn't shape up soon, I'm going to divorce him."

Chapter 2

The search for a better life in California proved fruitless. Disillusioned, Mama and Norman moved back to Oklahoma. Mama, also hoping for a new beginning in her marriage, bluntly told Norman she would not tolerate his infidelity any longer.

"Either you stop seeing other women, or our marriage is history," she said grimly.

When he did not change, Mama carried through on her threat, filing for a divorce and moving in with her parents.

Sandi was the pride and joy of Grandpa Gilmore's life, and she readily accepted all the love he lavished on her. Although she was too young to put it into words, she felt secure living in Grandpa and Grandma's house.

Taken along to court for Mama's divorce hearing, Sandi was both confused and frightened by the proceedings. The judge, formidable in his long black robe, sat behind a high desk asking questions of Mama and Daddy who sat on opposite sides of the room. Sandi knew they were talking about her but could not understand the terms *custody* and *child support*.

When they left court, Sandi heard Mama say, "Good riddance! We'll see no more of him." Sandi understood that Daddy would not be around anymore and Mama was glad.

Although Norman did not grieve long over his failed marriage, he did love his daughter and wanted to see her. But when he failed to make his child support payments, Mama decided to move back to California for revenge.

With little Sandi at her side, Mama wearily trudged up the sidewalk, turned in at a modest white house, and rang the bell. A middle-aged woman answered her ring.

"Is Gladys home?" Mama asked.

Without answering, the woman turned and called, "Gladys, somebody's here to see you."

"Karin!" the young woman exclaimed as she came to the door. "Come on in! Since when are you back in California?"

"Since just now," Mama laughed wearily.

"Really? Well sit down and tell me what's been happening," Gladys invited. "How about a cold beer?"

"You bet," Mama accepted the offer gladly. "I forgot how hot it can be in California this time of year."

Sandi fell asleep with her head on Mama's lap while the two caught up on the events of the past months.

"To make a long story short," Mama said, pulling an ashtray over to where she could reach it, "we all went back to Oklahoma when Norman and Ralph couldn't find jobs out here. I didn't see it before we were married, but Norman was a spoiled little rich boy. His parents gave him anything he wanted and didn't expect him to behave. He'd do things like shooting out the lights of passing trains just for kicks, and his parents always bailed him out when he got in trouble. He wanted to go through life partying and having a good time. You know Norman!

"Anyway, when we went back to Oklahoma, I told Norman he had to stop his running around and change his ways, or I'd divorce him and take Sandi with me. He got mad and we had a big fight. So I got a divorce and got custody of Sandi. He was ordered to pay child support, but he doesn't pay it. So I decided to forget him and come back to California and see if I can make it on my own."

"Where are you going to stay?" Gladys asked.

"I don't know. I don't have any money. Norman didn't have anything, so I didn't get anything out of the divorce except getting rid of the bum." Mama swore. "That's why I came here. I thought maybe you would know where I could get a job or a place to live. I only have a couple bucks on me, so it has to be cheap. And even then I don't know how I'm going to make it."

"Finding a job might not be too hard if you're

not too fussy about what kind of job it is," Gladys said thoughtfully. "But what will you do with your little girl while you work?"

"I don't know," Mama answered with another oath. Tears filled her eyes as she ground the stub of her cigarette in the ashtray. "Here I am, only 21 years old and already divorced, with a three-year-old to take care of and no money. I just don't know how I'm going to make it."

"Tell you what," Gladys suggested brightly. "We have an empty room. I'll ask Mom if you can stay here a few weeks until you get on your feet."

Gladys's mother agreed it was the ideal solution for their immediate needs. It would provide shelter and a built-in baby sitter for Sandi until Karin could get established.

Mama picked up the sleeping Sandi and laid her on the bed in the room Gladys showed her. The child stirred in her sleep but did not awaken. She was too young to question the situation. With the simplicity of a child, she trusted her mother and accepted things as they came.

Going into the kitchen, Mama picked up the morning newspaper and spread it out on the table, searching the ads for a job possibility. She circled a few she thought were worth looking into. So intent was she on the paper that she did not notice the heavy steps of a man coming down the hall and into the room. Feeling, rather than seeing, his eyes upon her, she straightened up. His eyes mirrored questions and intrigue.

Mama held out her hand. "I don't believe we've met," she smiled into the eyes that measured her. "I am Karin. And you are—?"

"Brian Brown," the young man answered. "But everybody calls me Skip."

"Oh! I see you two have met," Gladys observed, coming in and letting the door close with a bang behind her.

"We were working on it," Skip conceded, "until we were so rudely interrupted. Perhaps you'd like to do it up properly," he quipped.

"All right," Gladys giggled. Clearing her throat she intoned formally, "Mr. Brown, meet my friend Karin Hackman. Ms. Hackman, meet my step-brother, Brian Brown, alias Skip."

"Pleased to meet you," Skip bowed.

"Likewise," Mama returned, smiling in amusement.

"And to which of the gods do I give credit for your appearance here?" Skip inquired.

"He could hardly be called a god," Mama muttered, giving Skip one of her well-practiced helpless looks. "I just got a divorce from a selfish brute and came West to try to make it on my own. I have a little girl to support. I was just looking in the ads for a job."

"She's going to stay with us until she can get on her feet," Gladys put in.

"You're welcome, I'm sure," Skip said warmly.

"Where's the little girl?"

"She's taking a nap," Mama said. "From Oklahoma to California is a long trip for a three-year-old."

"Is she as pretty as you?" Skip asked.

"Prettier," Mama laughed. She knew he was flirting and she enjoyed it. "She's got curly blonde hair."

"May I have a peek at her?" Skip asked.

"Sure," Mama consented with a nod of her head. "But don't wake her up. She's in your sister's room."

"What a nice little bonus!" Skip murmured to himself, instantly losing his heart as he gazed at the sleeping little girl lying on the bed. "A fair lady and a curly-haired little girl."

The product of a broken home himself, Skip dreamed of having a real family of his own. This pretty, young divorcee with a little girl intrigued him. If he married her, he could have an "instant" family.

The idea of being a father somehow gave Skip a sense of purpose and feeling of fulfillment. He enjoyed playing with Sandi and bringing lollipops home for her. Sometimes it almost seemed he was courting her instead of her mother.

On the way home from a movie one night, Skip suddenly said, "Let's get married, Karin."

Mama looked up at him quickly. "Give me one good reason why we should."

"Because I love you. I want a wife. You need a husband. And Sandi needs a daddy," Skip answered. "There! That's four good reasons. If you marry me, you can quit working. I'll take care of you and Sandi, and you won't have to grub the way you are now. What do you say?"

Mama stopped, put her arms around Skip's neck, and looked up into his eyes. "I say yes, Skip. You're right. I'm so helpless with this little girl. I need you."

Since a large wedding seemed improper the second time around, the whirlwind courtship culminated in a simple marriage ceremony at the office of the local Justice of the Peace. The newlyweds immediately went east to Nebraska to live with Skip's sister.

"I don't like it here," Mama complained to Skip after a few weeks in Nebraska. "Do we have to stay here?"

"What do you want to do? Go back to California?" Skip asked.

"No! I want to go home to my parents and twin sister. I miss my sister dreadfully. Can't we go to Oklahoma?" Mama pleaded mournfully.

"One place is as good as another to me," Skip shrugged. "I'm not hard to get along with."

Although Sandi only faintly remembered Grandpa and Grandma Gilmore when she met them again in Oklahoma, she was happy to see Aunt Carmen. The twin sisters had spent so much

12

time together in Sandi's short life that Sandi considered both of them her mother. It annoyed Mama when Sandi called Aunt Carmen "Mama."

Sandi did not understand the causes for their frequent moves, and the continual disruptions created an underlying confusion. The security of a stable environment was unknown to her.

Chapter 3

S andi chased Robbie around the car parked in the back alley. The children had caught Skip and Uncle Ralph's excitement over the '65 Pontiac GTO.

"What a find!" Skip exclaimed, rubbing his hand lovingly over the shiny front fender.

"And I suppose you found it the same place you found the others?" Mama more stated than asked.

Uncle Ralph winked and said with a laugh, "Not the same place, but the same way—which is what you meant."

"You guys are going to keep on until you get caught," Aunt Carmen said, knowing full well this car had been stolen—as had all the other cars and cycles they had brought home.

"Oh, no! We're too smart for that," Skip chuckled. "We move these babies too fast to get caught."

Just as Skip took a step backwards, Robbie rounded the corner and charged into Skip headfirst. Bouncing backwards, Robbie slammed against the ground hard enough to knock the breath out of him. Sandi, moving too fast to stop, sprawled across him. Her hands scooted over the stones, painfully scraping off the skin. Their screams split the evening sky.

"Shut up!" Mama commanded fiercely, clapping her hand over her daughter's mouth and scooping her off the ground. "You'll have the whole neighborhood running out here to see who's yelling bloody murder."

Aunt Carmen, muffling Robbie's screams, marched toward the house. "Come on in and we'll have a drink," she called over her shoulder to the men.

The men took their time. They congratulated themselves again on their stroke of good luck in getting the sleek GTO. It would turn a handsome profit.

By the time they entered the house, the screaming children had been quieted and were on their way to bed. Aunt Carmen set out some snacks to go with the beers. Uncle Ralph had a greater tolerance for alcohol than some, and he never got drunk. But alcohol loosened his tongue.

"I've been casing out that warehouse on Grant Street," Uncle Ralph said. "I'm ready to make a move if you are."

"What's the scoop?" Skip asked.

"I got 'em all figured out. The secretary goes to the bank every Thursday afternoon," Uncle Ralph began to explain his plan. "You'd never believe it, but she takes the dough in a brown paper bag and goes in her own car. Anybody could hit 'er over the head and be gone with the bag before she knew what happened."

"You ain't plannin' on doing that are you?" Skip looked at his brother-in-law skeptically.

"Nah!" Uncle Ralph laughed shortly. "We don't have to work that hard. Look! If she goes to the bank only on Thursdays, then there has to be a pile of dough there every Wednesday night. So we'll do like we did before. You pick the locks to get us in the place, and I'll crack the safe in the office. We'll be out of there and home free without laying a finger on anybody."

"How much do you think we'll clean up on this job?" Skip asked.

"I can't tell you that till I see inside the safe," said Uncle Ralph, tilting his head back to drain the last drops of beer. "But I'm sure there has to be a couple thousand for each of us."

"We make a great team—thanks to my natural ability to pick locks and your know-how for safe cracking," Skip chortled.

"Uncle Nate taught me well," Ralph replied. "What say we hit 'em next Wednesday?"

"I'm with you," Skip agreed. "Sure beats working!"

The two sisters, busy with their own conversation, largely ignored the men's talk. Both were well aware of the men's activities, and they didn't really like it, being less confident of the men's abilities.

But they also knew it was useless to try stop their husbands. The brothers-in-law, buddies as well as relatives, seemed to thrive on the challenge and thrill of their misadventures.

The robbery of the warehouse went off as planned. The two men came home gloating over the sizable booty. But their success only fed an uncontrollable desire for more easy money. The wives, although not entirely approving, didn't hesitate to share in the benefits.

Though the two men always covered their trails carefully, they were also smart enough to know they would eventually become suspects. What was first an uneasy feeling developed into sure knowledge that they were indeed being watched by the authorities.

"You know, I've been thinking." Skip said to Uncle Ralph one day as he bounced Sandi on his knee. "We ought to take a vacation."

"Vacation?" Uncle Ralph questioned.

"Yeah, vacation," Skip repeated. "I don't like the way things look around here. We'd be smart to get out of here and lay low for awhile. You know what's been happening; they're getting on to us. And if they get one of us, they'll get us both. What do you say we head out to California for awhile? We have enough stashed up to make a nice little trip out of it and see the sights along the way while we're at it."

"You're right," Uncle Ralph agreed. "Things are

getting tight, and it's time to skip the country. California's as good a place to go as any."

When they proposed the "vacation," their wives readily agreed. They all knew they really were running from the law, although no one said so openly. The more quietly they left town, the better were their chances of escaping.

Sandi and Robbie could not help but feel the tension as their parents quietly loaded the cars after dark that night and headed out of town. Skip drove with an eye constantly on the rear-view mirror, watching for police cars. When they were safely out of town, he took country roads rather than the well-traveled highways.

"We're seeing more of the country this way," the men agreed over their lunch the next day at a "greasy spoon" cafe in a sleepy little town.

As the days passed and they traveled west without incident, the tension gradually lessened, but the men never dropped their guard. They tried to keep from being seen in public places or doing anything which would attract attention.

Too young to understand everything, Sandi and Robbie accepted the "vacation" story without question. They thought the trip was a wonderful adventure.

It was exciting to Sandi to drive up the winding mountainous road from Colorado Springs to the summit of Pikes Peak. Even though it was summer, the air was cold on top of the mountain.

To Sandi, the city looked like a toy town far below.

From Colorado, the "tourists" wandered down to New Mexico and bought tickets to go through the enormous Carlsbad Caverns. Sandi held tightly to her mother's hand as they descended the slope into the yawning, dark mouth of the cave's entrance. She wrinkled her nose at the stench of droppings left by hordes of bats that lived just inside the opening.

Part way down, the guide snapped off the lights, and instantly the cavern was incredibly dark. Sandi cried out in fear and clung tightly to her mother's hand until the lights were turned on again.

Carlsbad Caverns was full of beautiful formations, but Sandi grew bored and tired from the long walk. To her, the only worthwhile thing about the whole excursion was the cafeteria at the bottom of the cavern where they ate a box lunch while they rested.

Walking through the caverns took several hours. Mama, heavy with her second child, puffed from the exertion of walking uphill on the way out. Sandi was glad to be back in the warm sunshine again. The adults' exclamations about the underground wonders meant little to her.

"You all go stand over there and let me take your picture," Aunt Carmen said, pointing to the cavern's sign at the entrance of the parking lot.

"Not me," Uncle Ralph objected.

"Or me," Skip echoed.

"Oh, come on!" Aunt Carmen scoffed. "Don't be so jittery. No one will notice us. I want a picture to help us remember our trip here."

Mama lined everyone up in front of the sign. But the men, uneasy that someone might notice them, ducked to hide their faces just as Aunt Carmen snapped the picture.

The "vacationers" continued to amble slowly across the West and finally arrived in California. They found small apartments close together and settled down—after a fashion. Money, which came from undisclosed sources, went through their pockets as rapidly as it came. Although they always were well dressed and drove sporty late-model cars, their rent and utility bills did not get paid. Neither family lived long in one place as they moved from one apartment to another to escape their creditors. The trail of unpaid bills did not concern them. They figured it was a dog-eat-dog world, and the rule to live by was: "Do unto others before they do unto you."

Chapter 4

Sandi padded softly out to the kitchen in her bare feet. Although it was mid-morning, everyone else was still asleep. She knew better than to waken her mother. Mama said a big, four-year-old girl could get her own breakfast. Opening the refrigerator, she looked for something to eat.

Hot dogs! That was it! She loved hot dogs. She would make one for her breakfast.

Laying the pack of hot dogs on the table, Sandi rummaged in the drawer for a paring knife. Finding one, she jabbed a hole in the vacuum pack and drew the knife toward her, slitting the package. Suddenly the knife slipped, and with lightning swiftness, plunged into her left eye.

"Mama! Mama!" Sandi shrieked, running to her mother's bedroom and bursting through the door.

"You little—!" Mama's angry words were cut short by the gruesome sight in the doorway.

"Sandi! What did you do?" Mama shouted.

The horrified look on her mother's face told Sandi she was in trouble.

"What were you doing?" Mama shouted again.

"I was just trying to open some hot dogs," Sandi wailed. "I don't know what happened. The knife just went in my eye, that's all."

"Of all the . . ." Mama began. Leaving the sentence unfinished, she swore. "I've got to get you to a doctor," she snapped, flinging clothing aside in search of something fit to wear.

Frantically, Mama dialed her twin's number. "Carmen, Help me! Sandi got a knife in her eye," she gasped. "What shall I do?"

Sandi began to scream, more fearful of a beating, than because of the pain in her eye.

"Will you shut up! I can't hear," Mama snapped. "Now, what did you say?" she shouted into the phone.

"I said I don't know," Aunt Carmen repeated. "I suppose she should go to an eye doctor. Let me look in the yellow pages to see where the nearest one is."

Mama turned back to Sandi. "SHUT UP!" she said again, emphasizing each word separately. Her finger traced the list of optometrists in the yellow pages and found the one Aunt Carmen suggested.

After jerking a clean shirt over Sandi's head and jamming her legs into clean pants, Mama raced to the car with her little daughter in tow. Dr. Carver saw them immediately even though they arrived unannounced and unscheduled.

"I may be able to help your daughter," the

doctor began. "A down payment will be required today which can be refunded to you by your insurance company. What insurance do you carry?"

"None," Mama answered.

"But you will be able to pay the fee?" he questioned.

"I have no money," Mama sniffled. "We just arrived in town a few weeks ago. My husband has not been able to get a job yet."

"I see," Dr. Carver said slowly. "You know, I think it might be best for you to go to the hospital emergency room. They are better equipped to handle injuries like this than I am. See what they say. If they won't help you, come back and I'll do what I can."

"I understand perfectly," Mama snapped, giving him a venomous look.

Arriving at the hospital, Sandi was whisked into an examining room while Mama filled out the necessary forms. Treatment here did not depend on her ability to pay. By the time she joined Sandi again, the child had already been examined and sent to prepare for surgery.

"How long ago did this happen?" Dr. Stienmetz asked Mama when she met him outside the examining room door.

"I don't know," Mama hesitated. "About an hour or two."

"This is a very serious injury," Dr. Stienmetz said gravely. "Behind the cornea of the eye is the anterior chamber. It contains a clear fluid called the aqueous humor. If this chamber is punctured, the fluid can leak out of the eye and cause blindness unless it receives immediate attention. With the amount of time that has passed, I'm afraid we're too late. But we're taking her into surgery immediately, and we'll do what we can to save the eye."

When Sandi awoke after surgery, she opened her unbandaged eye and saw Mama and Aunt Carmen beside her bed. She lay quietly, looking at the unfamiliar surroundings as the memory of the knife came back. Her little hand reached up and touched the bandage over her left eye. Still groggy from the sedation, she closed her eye and drifted back to sleep again.

The two women stood up as the surgeon entered the room. "How is she, Doctor?" Mama asked anxiously.

"I can't tell you for sure at this point," the doctor avoided giving a direct answer. "We have done the best we can. In a few days we will take the bandage off and find out how much vision is left. We'll be keeping her here for the present."

Sandi adapted well to being in the hospital. Not feeling ill, she played happily in the toy room and loved all the attention she got from the nurses.

"Your mama wants to talk to you," one of the nurses said as she handed the phone to Sandi one morning.

"Sandi," Mama's voice came over the wire. "I have some good news for you. You have a baby sister. How do you like that?"

"Where did you get her?" Sandi asked without answering Mama's question.

"I am in another part of the hospital," Mama said. "She was just born this morning. Her name is Sylvia. She has dark curly hair and big brown eyes."

"Can I see her?" Sandi asked.

"Not now," Mama answered.

"You can bring the baby and come to my room," Sandi suggested.

"No, I can't do that," Mama said.

"But I want you to come and be with me," Sandi pleaded. "There is an empty bed in my room. You can have it."

"The nurses wouldn't let me," Mama explained. "I have to stay in another part of the hospital. You be a good girl and do what the nurses tell you. Soon we can both go home, and then you can see the baby."

"Okay," Sandi agreed, although she was not pleased. She had no idea how long it would be until she could see her new baby sister. Hearing Mama's voice made her realize how much she missed her mother. She wanted to go home!

Chapter 5

Since Mama was home with Sylvia, Aunt Carmen was with Sandi when Dr. Stienmetz slowly peeled the bandage from the injured eye. Aunt Carmen sucked in her breath. Sandi's eye stared blankly.

"What do you see?" Dr. Stienmetz asked, holding a picture book in front of Sandi.

"A puppy," Sandi answered.

"What do you see now?" the doctor asked again, holding an index card over the uninjured eye.

"Dark," Sandi replied.

"And now?" he asked, covering the injured eye.

"A puppy," Sandi answered.

"I'm sorry," Dr. Stienmetz said, turning to Aunt Carmen. "It is as I feared. Too much time elapsed between the injury and treatment. The eye has been permanently damaged, and she will never be able to see with it again."

"You poor darling," Aunt Carmen cried, sweeping Sandi into her arms.

"I will give her an eye patch to wear for about a week," Dr. Stienmetz said as he scribbled a note.

"That will help keep it clean until the wound is totally healed. Since there is nothing more we can do, you may take her home tomorrow."

Sandi waited eagerly for Aunt Carmen to come and take her home the next morning. Aunt Carmen had temporarily moved in with her sister and taken over the household until Mama could care for her girls again. Although she was only a few minutes older than Karin, Carmen was clearly the leader of the two, and Mama was often grateful for her sister's ability to take charge.

Aunt Carmen called Grandpa and Grandma Gilmore in Oklahoma with the tragic news of Sandi's injury. Wanting both to see the new baby and to comfort Sandi, they made the long three-day drive to California.

Sandi, wearing a silver eye patch, was at the door to greet her grandparents when they arrived.

"You poor dear!" Grandma said in a voice full of pity. She caught Sandi up in her arms and kissed her, then passed her into Grandpa's arms for more sympathy. Although she did not understand their dismay, it made her feel important to be pitied.

"And how do you like your new baby sister?" Grandma asked.

"Fine," Sandi grinned. "Wanna see her?"

"Sure thing," Grandma said. "That's one of the reasons we came."

"Oh, just look at all that dark curly hair!" Grandma exclaimed when Mama brought Sylvia out to be admired. The baby's big brown eyes looked solemnly up at her grandmother.

"She doesn't look at all like Sandi," Grandma remarked.

"No," Mama agreed. "Sandi is light and Sylvia is dark. They both look like their fathers. Neither looks like me."

While Grandma fussed over Sylvia, Sandi sat comfortably on Grandpa's lap. She was quite proud of her baby sister and felt no jealousy at the attention Sylvia was getting. Besides, she had gotten attention first.

"How would you like to go to Disney World?" Grandpa asked Sandi.

"Oooh! Can we?" Sandi squealed.

"Tomorrow," Grandpa promised.

Sandi clapped her hands in rapture. She had never been to Disney World, but she had seen ads on TV. Every child she knew longed to go there someday.

When they walked through the gates of the Magic Kingdom the next morning, Sandi was entranced. There were rides to take and foods to eat. Her doting grandfather had come prepared to grant her every whim. She gorged on the hot dogs and cotton candy he bought her.

"Say! What happened to your eye?" the balloon man asked as he handed Sandi the balloon Grandpa bought for her.

"I got a knife in it," Sandi answered bluntly. By

now, she was used to the question. It had been asked many times during the course of the day, for the silver eye patch distinguished her from other four-year-old girls.

"Oh, my!" The balloon man squatted down so he would be on her level. "How did that ever happen?" he asked soberly.

"I was trying to open a pack of hot dogs," Sandi explained. "The knife slipped and went into my eye."

"That's too bad," the balloon man said, shaking his head.

"I was in the hospital," Sandi informed him importantly. She had learned that telling the story brought her a lot of sympathy and attention.

"Little girls shouldn't use sharp knives," the balloon man warned. "You'll remember that, won't you?"

Sandi nodded.

"Good girl," he said, patting her on the shoulder and standing up to serve his next customer.

The day at Disney World passed quickly. Sandi was not ready to leave when Grandpa said it was time to go home. Grandpa and Grandma made every day of that week in California a wonderful time. Grandma helped with the new baby and the housework. She bought food and new clothes. One day they went to Knotts Berry Farm and came home with boxes of delicious fresh strawberries and lovely jars of red jam.

Much too soon, the week was over, and Grandpa Gilmores headed back to Oklahoma. Not until she was older would Sandi realize how badly they felt about her loss of sight, or that Grandpas' generosity was their way of trying to make up for that loss. She did not consider it a tragedy to be blind in one eye as long as she could still see out of the other. To her, the week had been a wonderful adventure.

Chapter 6

"Karin," Aunt Carmen whispered urgently, shaking her sleeping sister. "Wake up! Phone for you. It's the cops."

Mama groaned, then sat up with a jerk as her sister's words sank into her consciousness. "The cops?" she gasped. "What happened?"

"Search me," Aunt Carmen shrugged. "He asked for Mrs. Brown."

Mama was at the phone in an instant. She knew Skip was in trouble. He and Ralph had gone to rob another warehouse safe. After careful planning, they had decided that tonight was the night. Tension mounted as Mama spoke to the police.

"What happened?" It was Aunt Carmen's turn to ask the question as Mama hung up the phone.

"I don't know what went wrong, but Skip and Ralph were caught," Mama said. "Skip is in the hospital. They want me to go in to sign consent forms for emergency surgery for him."

"What about Ralph?" Aunt Carmen asked.

"They didn't say, and I didn't ask," Mama said. "Maybe he got away. But I've got to get to the hospital right away."

"I'll go with you," Aunt Carmen offered. "The kids are all sleeping. They'll never know we're gone."

At the hospital, Mama signed the forms and was then allowed to see Skip for a few minutes before he was taken into surgery.

"What happened?" Mama whispered.

"They caught us," Skip whispered back. "We were trying to get out of there. The first thing I knew the cops had us surrounded. One of 'em yelled, 'Stop, or I'll shoot!' I tried to jump the fence and he shot me in the back." Skip swore.

"Where's Ralph?" Mama asked.

"They got him," Skip swore. "He stopped when they yelled, and they got him. Probably in the jug by now. Man! I wish they'd knock me out. This pain is killing me."

"All right, Mr. Brown," an orderly interrupted, "they are ready for you in surgery." Turning to Mama, he said, "You may wait in the lobby."

Skip was fortunate that the bullet's path through his lower back did not do permanent damage. His injuries, however, did require a temporary colostomy, which was a great nuisance to him.

The sisters managed to post bail for their husbands and brought them home. With seven people, the little apartment was crowded, but they had lived in crowded conditions so often they hardly thought about it. The women knew it was quite possible both men would get jail sentences. In that event, they would rather live together than separately. Further, they could not afford separate apartments, because money would be scarce.

When Ralph and Skip's case came to trial, the verdicts were as they had feared. Caught in the act, both were found guilty and sentenced to several years in a maximum security prison. Skip's sentence was longer than Ralph's because he had attempted escape. The day was set for them to begin serving their sentences, and they returned home to await its arrival.

When the dreaded moment arrived, a loud, commanding knock sounded on the door. Everyone looked silently at the others, but no one moved.

The knock was repeated, louder this time. Aunt Carmen opened the door. Sandi stared in awe at the police officers who entered. The holstered guns hanging from their belts silently testified to their grim authority.

"Mr. Brown and Mr. McArthur," one of the officers addressed the two men. "We are here to take you to the County Prison to begin serving your sentences."

The officer snapped handcuffs on the men's wrists. They had known this moment was coming, but now that it had arrived, it was more difficult than they had imagined. The sisters, with their large-eyed children clustered around them, wept as reality hit them: their husbands were common criminals. Hearing their mothers cry, the children added their wails to the tearful chorus.

"This way, please," one of the officers commanded crisply, opening the door.

"Please," Skip implored of the officer, "may I say good-by to my little girl?"

The officer nodded his consent.

Skip knelt down, took Sandi's small hand in his handcuffed one, and looked seriously into her eyes. "I'm sorry, but I must go away for awhile because I have been bad," he said as tears ran down his cheeks. "I'll come back as soon as I can. You be a good girl. When you grow up, don't ever do what I did."

Sandi's wails crescendoed into wild weeping as Skip spoke. She did not understand what this was all about, but she knew it must be awful. The police had come to take him away, and he was crying. She knew men were not supposed to cry. He must have been very bad.

Skip squeezed Sandi's hand with both of his and stood up.

He looked at her sadly, and then turned to go with the officers.

Sandi flung herself on the sofa, crying for Skip as the door closed behind him.

Chapter 7

Mama and Aunt Carmen had no intentions of sitting quietly at home, waiting for their husbands to be released from prison. They meant to enjoy themselves in the meantime, so both obtained divorces for the freedom to have other men.

With two little girls to care for, Mama took up ironing at home for a source of income. Aunt Carmen found a job as a barmaid. This not only provided much needed cash, but also put her in contact with many men who were more than willing to come home with her. Although there was never enough money, there were plenty of boyfriends.

Lonnie Loose was one of the men who followed Aunt Carmen home. Mama seemed to feel deprived without a man in the house, and since Lonnie was attracted to her, he soon moved in with them. Although he showed less interest in being a father than Skip did, he treated the children well. Lonnie contributed little to the household income, so the sisters continued to work as they had before. Sandi accepted his presence matter-of-factly. To her, he was just another in the succession of men who had come and gone in her short lifetime.

Sandi sat on the floor near the ironing board as Mama wearily pushed the iron back and forth over another shirt. She had been ironing all afternoon and her feet hurt. Finishing the shirt, she set the iron down with a thump and reached for a hanger.

"I am so sick of this," Mama complained to Sandi. "I work like a dog all day ironing for rich people; and for what? I'm still as poor as a church mouse. If it weren't for the welfare checks and surplus foods from the government, I don't know what you kids would eat."

It was nothing new to Sandi to hear Mama complain of being poor. Aunt Carmen often complained of it too. But Sandi was too young to realize what a difficult time the mothers were having providing for their children. Not yet in school, she had little contact outside her own home and did not realize the difference between her life and the lives of other children her age.

"I'm going back home," Aunt Carmen announced one day. "I'm sick of always being broke, and things are not going to get any better. I called Dad, and he said he'd send me the money for a train ticket."

"I wish you wouldn't," Mama objected. "But I know it's no use trying to change your mind once you've decided to do something."

"You'll make out all right without me," Aunt Carmen insisted. "Lonnie will take care of you."

"Yeah, right," Mama mocked. "Me and three children? Sylvia will barely be a year old until my next one is born."

Life grew more difficult with Aunt Carmen gone. Mama was not only left to make her own decisions, but she had lost her best friend and confidant as well. Her pregnancy complicated matters, curtailing her social life and preventing her from finding a job outside the home. Although it brought in far less money than she needed, she continued ironing.

"Sandi," Mama called from the ironing board one hot summer day, "go to the store and get me a chocolate cherry ice cream bar."

"Okay," Sandi agreed quickly, hoping this was one of the times when there would be enough money to buy ice cream for them both.

"You can get something for yourself too," Mama said, handing Sandi a few coins.

Mama often sent Sandi to the little store only a block away from the modern white apartment complex where they lived. The tall palm trees lining the street spread their branches like angel's wings over the head of the little girl as she made her way alone down the sidewalk. Thoroughly drilled on the evils of men and strangers, she never spoke to anyone on the street or in the store except Mr. Duncan, the owner.

Sandi was dismayed to find the little Snack Shack filled with workmen from the Ford Motor plant across the road. A long line of men stood outside waiting to get in. Sandi stopped short and stood, staring, trying to decide what to do. She badly wanted to get the ice cream, especially since Mama had given her money to get some for herself this time, but she was afraid of all the "bad" men.

I won't let Mama down, Sandi decided. *I'm a big girl. I'll be brave and go in there anyway.*

Squaring her shoulders, Sandi marched into the store, ignoring the men. Making her way to the ice cream case, she found the ice cream bar Mama wanted. It did not take her long to choose her own; she always got a rainbow pop because she liked the pretty colors. Going to the end of the line, she stood quietly, bravely waiting her turn.

"Hey, Al!" Sandi heard someone call, "let this little girl go first."

"Sure," the man called Al said from the head of the line, motioning Sandi to the front.

Sandi tossed her head, and gave him a dark look that clearly said, "Don't you dare touch me." He grinned at her, then shrugged and turned away. Several more men tried to talk to her and offered their places in line, but she refused to speak to any of them. None of those bad men was going to get a chance at her!

Finally, it was Sandi's turn at the cash register.

Mr. Duncan gave an understanding smile as the frightened little girl stretched up to give him her coins. She turned and nearly ran to the door. Once outside, fear that one of the bad men would follow her home lent wings to her feet. She was also afraid Mama would be angry that it had taken her so long to get the ice cream.

"I couldn't help it, Mama," Sandi panted as she opened the door of the apartment. "The store was full of bad men, and I had to wait a long time for my turn. They tried to talk to me and told me to go first, but I didn't listen to them, and I didn't talk to any of them," she reported proudly.

"They weren't bad men," Mama corrected. "They were probably just there on their lunch break to get something to eat. They were trying to be nice. You should have let them be kind to you."

Humph! Sandi thought to herself. *That's how you get in trouble. You let men be nice to you. Men are all bad, and I am not going to be so stupid.*

Lonnie Loose moved out of their lives as easily as he had moved in. Not having married spared them the expense of a divorce. Left alone with her girls, Mama turned more and more to the temporary relief of alcohol as her method of coping with life's difficulties.

Mama often left Sandi to assume responsibility for both herself and Sylvia. Only five, Sandi mothered her baby sister the best she could.

Liquor made Mama violent. She fought with the

men she dated and stormed at her little daughters for minor infractions, real or imagined. Life became a constant turmoil of fear.

"What am I going to do?" Mama wept in dismay as she lay on her bed, sober for a change.

"What's the matter, Mama?" Sandi asked sympathetically.

"Oh, everything! Just everything," Mama wept. "If Skip would get out of jail, I'm sure things would get better. We really need him, and I miss him so much. None of the men that hang around here are as good as Skip. He was a good daddy to you girls, and we had good times together."

"Maybe if you stopped drinking things would get better," Sandi offered.

Mama laughed hollowly. "That's easy for you to say. You don't know what it's like. Liquor is the only friend I've got anymore. Everybody else let me down."

Sheri was born about a week after Sylvia's first birthday. Since Sandi was attending kindergarten, Mama was left at home with the two babies every morning. Burdened with her responsibilities, she grew more and more resentful of the way life seemed to be treating her. Instead of admitting her troubles were of her own making, she laid the blame on everyone else. She felt she had reached the end of her rope with no hope in sight.

After six months of struggling on her own, Mama did the only thing she knew to do; she called her father and asked him for money to go home to Oklahoma. Grandpa Gilmore knew three girls were more than Mama could handle alone, so he sent enough money for all of them to fly home.

Mama wanted to go so badly she simply walked out of the desolate apartment, leaving everything. All she could think of was going home and letting someone else take over her load of responsibilities.

Sandi sat with Mama in the airport, waiting for their flight. It was late, and they had been waiting for what seemed like hours and hours. Just having learned to walk, Sylvia refused to stay sitting. She continually toddled off exploring, and Sandi was kept busy running after her. Mama was so desperate to get home she had not even thought to bring extra milk or diapers for Sheri. Naturally, the baby could not understand the delay and her fretfulness soon escalated into insistent wails. Mama walked the floor trying to quiet her, getting more and more frustrated and angry.

"She's hungry, Mama. Give her a bottle," Sandi advised.

"I don't have any," Mama snapped. "Shut up and sit down."

Hurt, embarrassed, and angry, Sandi retreated to a seat. She pulled little Sylvia after her and hoisted her up onto her lap. *What a mess! Why had Mama not thought far enough to bring milk for Sheri? Whatever would they do?*

A pretty lady, dressed in a dark blue dress suit

41

and a matching hat came over to Mama. "Is there something I can do for you?" she asked kindly.

"We've had to wait so long that I ran out of milk and diapers," Mama lamented, her eyes filling with tears.

"Oh, I'm sorry," the lady said. "Is your baby a boy or girl?"

"A girl."

"How old is she?"

"Six months."

"She's so cute. The poor thing. I'll get some milk and diapers for you," the kind lady said as she hurried away.

When she returned, she looked at Sandi and Sylvia, "Are these your girls too?"

"Yes," Mama said with a helpless look.

"You have been waiting a long time. I imagine you're hungry too, aren't you?" the kind lady asked the girls.

Sandi nodded wordlessly.

The lady went off again and soon came back with a meal for the girls.

"Thank you," Sandi said with a look of adoration. At that moment, she loved the lady with all her heart. She would never forget her or her kindness.

"Is there anything else you need?" the lady asked Mama.

"I sure could use a smoke," Mama sighed wistfully.

The lady bought cigarettes for Mama, who moved within reach of an ashtray and lit up. With the girls fed and the baby sleeping, she could relax, knowing they would make it now until the plane left. And when they got to Oklahoma, things would finally straighten out and get better.

Chapter 8

Things did improve after they got back to Oklahoma. Mama and the girls moved in with Grandpa and Grandma Gilmore. Sandi loved the place because it was familiar, and she felt safe. The suburban house had three bedrooms and two bathrooms. Best of all, there was a fenced yard behind it. Instead of being confined in a small apartment, the girls were free to play outdoors.

"You and the girls are welcome to live with us as long as you obey our rules," Grandpa told Mama firmly. "You must get a job to support yourself, and you must stay out of bars. And you may not bring any men home."

"I'll do anything you say, if you'll just help me out," Mama agreed quickly.

Grandpa was a night switchman for the Missouri-Pacific Railroad. He came home at 3:00 a.m. and always left his lunch box on the table with something good inside for Sandi to find when she got up. He wanted to sleep until nearly noon, and Grandma slept late too. Long used to feeding and dressing her little sisters, Sandi now also learned to keep them quiet until Grandpa and Grandma got up. The summer passed pleasantly for the girls in these familiar surroundings with Mama keeping her promise to Grandpa and abiding by his rules.

"Bedtime, Sandi," Mama called late one summer evening. "You must go to school tomorrow. Come and get a bath."

Sandi scrubbed herself in the tub while Mama shampooed in the washbowl.

"Grandma cannot take care of the little girls while you are in school," Mama said as she rinsed her hair. "So I got a baby sitter for them. I'll have to leave early to get them to the baby sitter before I go to work. You will have to get ready and go to school yourself. You can do that, can't you?"

"Yes," Sandi nodded her curly head. But she was not as confident as she pretended. The thought of walking to a strange school all alone was scary.

"Grandma showed you the way to the school. Don't cross the road until the crossing guard tells you it's all right. You are a big, six-year-old girl now. I know you can do it. And don't forget to pack a lunch to take along," Mama added.

When Sandi got up in the morning, the house was strangely empty and quiet. Even though she knew Grandpa and Grandma were asleep in their bedroom, she felt completely alone. She quietly dressed and combed herself, packed a small lunch, and ate a few cookies. By the time she was ready to leave the house, the enormity of her aloneness had overwhelmed her, and she started for school with tears in her eyes. The nearer she got, the more she cried. She wished she could stay home with her sisters. Everyone at school would be strangers.

The teacher was accustomed to homesick first graders. When Sandi's tear-streaked face appeared at her door, Miss Lee quickly sized up the situation and soon had the frightened little girl feeling more comfortable.

Leaving home the next day was less frightening because it was not a walk into the complete unknown. Getting herself ready and going to school alone soon became routine, but Sandi never forgot how frightening it had been to go alone the first day.

"Tomorrow is picture day," Miss Lee announced. "A man will come and take pictures of everyone. Wear nice clothes so you will look pretty on the pictures."

Sandi knew immediately she would wear her favorite dress with little red hearts all over it and puffy sleeves. The next morning she ironed it carefully. The sleeves were difficult, but she did the best she could. After combing her hair and fastening it with her favorite purple barrettes, she looked at her reflection in the mirror with satisfaction. Confident with her efforts, she swished grandly out the door, blissfully unaware of the frizzy-haired little girl with a wrinkled dress everyone else saw rather than the cute one she imagined herself to be.

When Sandi came home from school, she was surprised to see Skip. Even though he and Mama had gotten a divorce, they had written letters to each other while he was in prison. When he was released, he had also come to Oklahoma. Grandpa grudgingly consented to let him come in since he had been married to Mama before he had been jailed.

When Mama got home from work, Skip was anxious to go out and celebrate their reunion. Mama hummed as she got ready. She was as glad to see Skip again as he was to see her.

Sandi glanced through the half-open door as she passed the bedroom. Mama was applying lipstick. Skip placed his briefcase on the bed and flipped open the lid. Sandi stared in amazement. It was full of money! She had never seen so much money in her life.

"May I have one of your dollars?" Sandi asked impulsively.

Unaware that he was being watched, Skip's eyes snapped as he saw the little girl looking at him in eager anticipation.

"No!" he barked angrily. "Get lost and mind your own business."

47

He has so many dollars. Why wouldn't he give me just one? Sandi wondered as she walked slowly away, hurt by Skip's sharp refusal. Her childish reasoning did not consider where this money may have come from or why Skip would not want her to see it.

After Skip returned, Mama began drinking again and went back to her old ways. Grandpa reminded her of her agreement to abide by his rules if she was to live in his house. Those rules still stood. Mama got angry and argued loud and long with Grandpa, but he would not budge.

"Either you make a responsible mother of yourself or move out," Grandpa insisted. "I am not going to foot the bill for your reckless living."

"All right then! Have it your way!" Mama shouted. "I got along without you before, and I can again. I'll move out as soon as I find an apartment."

It was no idle threat. Within a few days, the girls were uprooted once more and moved to an apartment in another part of town. Sandi did not want to leave Grandpa. He was the only man who truly loved her, and the only one she had ever been able to trust. His house was the only place in which she had ever felt safe and secure.

Now that Skip was back with plenty of money, Mama did not need to work. She quit her job and life quickly shifted back into the same old pattern. Again she drank constantly, fighting and yelling at

48

everyone when she was drunk. Though glad to have Skip back, she fought with him daily over things of no consequence.

One summer day when the girls were alone, the phone rang. Sandi answered it.

"Is your mama home?" Skip's voice asked over the wire.

"No," Sandi answered. "She went to the store."

"Good," Skip said. "I'll be right over."

When Skip arrived, he told Sandi he was going to take the girls with him for a vacation. She gathered some clothes for all of them and a bottle for Sheri.

"Isn't Mama going to go with us?" Sandi asked.

"No," Skip snorted and swore. He angrily spouted something Sandi could not understand about teaching Mama a lesson and getting even with her for something, and then they were off.

As they rode away, Sandi was bewildered. She could not understand what this was all about. She knew only that Skip was taking them away, and she might never see Mama again.

Life with Skip was not very pleasant. In his anger he had not thought about life with three little girls under his care, nor was he prepared. Sheri soon emptied her bottle and howled for a refill. He had no milk. With three girls in tow, they made an emergency trip to the store.

The poor man! Sandi thought with a mixture of pity and amusement. *He doesn't know how to take*

49

care of little girls.

Mama soon guessed what had happened to the girls. When Mama called, Skip readily admitted he had them, and they argued heatedly over the phone. Mama pointed out she could have him arrested for kidnapping. He threatened to hurt her if she were foolish enough to file charges against him.

By the next day, Skip's fit of anger had cooled, and he began to regret his hasty action. He did not enjoy baby-sitting three girls day and night.

"Here you go," Skip barked with an oath at Mama when he returned the girls a few days later. "I'm skipping town. I don't need a harem."

Chapter 9

On the first day of second grade, Sandi found herself again walking alone to a new school. Although her stomach felt tied in knots, she was not quite as frightened as she had been going alone to first grade. This time she at least knew what to expect in a school day.

Miss Coy was young and kind. At recess, she often brushed Sandi's hair into a ponytail. Her gentle hands stroking Sandi's hair were comforting caresses to a love-starved little girl. Sandi loved Miss Coy, and school became a peaceful contrast to the turmoil at home.

"Miss Coy, I don't feel good," Sandi's trembling voice pleaded for help one day.

As Miss Coy looked into the flushed face of the little girl standing beside her desk, she put her cool hand on Sandi's forehead.

"Hm-m-m, I believe you have a fever," Miss Coy said. "I'll take you to the school nurse."

When the nurse popped a thermometer into Sandi's mouth, the red line shot up to 103.

"Your tonsils are badly swollen," the nurse said

after peering into Sandi's throat. "I'll call your mother and have her come for you."

Mama did not answer the phone. The nurse tried to call Grandma Gilmore, but again there was no answer.

"No one seems to be home," the nurse told Sandi. "You just lie here and rest. In another hour school will be over, and you can go home on the bus."

Sandi lay down gratefully. She ached all over and was so tired that she fell asleep immediately. When her bus came, the nurse took her out to meet it.

"This little girl is sick," the nurse told the bus driver as she helped Sandi onto the front seat. "I couldn't get through to her mother, so she's going home on the bus."

The driver nodded sympathetically at Sandi as she slumped down on the seat, too tired and miserable to sit up. The ride home seemed unbearably long, but at last the bus stopped at her house. She dragged herself off and into the house.

"I'm sick, Mama," Sandi whimpered, glad to see Mama was home. Her eyes filled with tears as she handed Mama the note the school nurse had sent home with her.

Mama scanned the note. "Well, go upstairs to bed," she said shortly.

Sandi trudged slowly up the steps and flopped onto her bed. Her little heart cried out for some motherly love and care. Miss Coy, the school nurse, and the bus driver had all shown more compassion than Mama.

"Mama, Mama," Sandi wailed, dragging herself from her bed and back to the head of the stairs.

"Sandi," Mama said sharply, coming to the foot of the stairs. "I am having a party tonight. My friends are coming, and you better not whine and carry on because I can't be bothered with you."

"Mama, Mama," Sandi's wails increased. "Come up and hold me."

"Sandi, stop crying," Mama shouted. "You'll just make yourself more sick. I don't want you throwing up. Now go back to bed and be quiet."

Knowing it was useless to beg Mama any longer, Sandi went back to her bed and buried her face in the pillow so Mama would not hear her crying.

The party was soon in full swing. Loud music, sounds of drinking and dancing, accompanied by riotous laughter drifted up to the sick little girl's bedroom. Forsaken and rejected, Sandi cried herself to sleep in exhaustion. This was not the first time, nor would it be the last, that Mama neglected her when Sandi desperately needed love and attention.

While things had been steadily growing worse for Mama, Aunt Carmen's life had taken a different turn. She and Uncle Ralph had been remarried after his prison sentence. Living near Mama, Aunt

Carmen saw her sister's life was rapidly heading the wrong direction. She often came to help Sandi with the little girls and was more of a mother to them than Mama was. Their close relationship infuriated Mama, because she knew it was the result of her own failure as a mother. Often she lashed out at Sandi with verbal and physical abuse.

"Karin, you have got to straighten out your life," Aunt Carmen said bluntly one day when she saw her sister slap Sandi across the face again in a flash of anger. "You are running yourself down and ruining your girls in the bargain."

"Oh, really?" Mama snapped sarcastically. "Since when are you an angel?"

"I know I've done a lot of things I shouldn't have," Aunt Carmen admitted. "I'm sorry for that. I have started going to church, and I have been learning a lot. I am a Christian now."

"You got religion?" Mama laughed.

"Not religion—peace with God," Aunt Carmen replied. "I know I was a sinner going to hell. But I repented and asked God to forgive me, and He did. I feel like a great load has been taken off my back."

"And you're telling me I'm going to hell?" Mama raged.

"The Bible says everyone has sinned and is going to hell unless he confesses his sin and trusts in Christ. When I did that, my life was changed; and I am truly happy for the first time in my life."

"That's fine for you," Mama said coldly, "but I am happy just the way I am. I don't need your religion, and I don't want you preaching at me. You always thought you were my boss because you're the oldest, but this is one time I'm not going to follow you. You live your life and I'll live mine."

"At least let me take Sandi to Sunday school with me," Aunt Carmen pleaded.

"No," Mama refused flatly. "She doesn't have time. She's practicing her mothering. She's thinks she's the Mother of the Year, you know."

"I wish you'd stop saying that," Aunt Carmen said. "You are always out drinking and running around with men. You don't take care of the little girls, so Sandi has to. And she does a good job of it too."

"Oh, yes!" Mama mocked, nodding at Sandi. "The Mother of the Year Award goes to Sandi Hackman."

Though she had heard this often, Sandi was cut to the heart. With tear-filled eyes, she ran from the room, away from Mama's scornful words.

Before the school year ended, Mama moved to a public housing project, and Sandi had to change schools again. Adjusting to a new teacher and classmates in mid-term was inconvenient, but the change in curriculum was worse because it made learning more difficult. By the time Sandi had become accustomed to the new school, she was far behind her classmates. Knowing she was at the foot of the class was humiliating and added to her feeling of incompetence.

The public housing project was not a nice place to live, but it was the only thing Mama could afford on welfare. The metal window frames leaked cold air, and flakes of paint fell off the walls and ceiling on top of everything. The rooms came furnished with a reeking combination of body odors, liquor, and stale smoke. Even worse, the place was full of wickedness and violence.

Mama went out every night. She would come home drunk, ready to fight with anyone and everyone. Sandi would lie on the bare mattress in the girls' room, holding her breath. Would Mama stumble to her own room or come into theirs and yell at them for some imagined wrong?

Once Mama and her younger sister, Tina, started fighting in the living room. Drunkenly they staggered around the room, turning it to shambles as they punched each other.

Sandi shoved her sisters into the kitchen for protection. They screamed in fear. She wanted to comfort them, but tears streamed down her own face as she watched the two grown women fighting. It was terrifying, but there was nothing she could do to stop them. When they finally stopped, exhausted, Sandi was weak with relief.

At night, Mama brought home a procession of boyfriends. They sweet-talked the girls, giving them candy and gifts before they were sent to their tiny bedroom. Sandi hated being locked in this bare little room for hours at a time. The boyfriend's bribes were soon gone or lost their charm. Then there was nothing for the little prisoners to do except listen to the sounds of merry-making on the other side of the door.

Night after night, after her little sisters had finally fallen asleep, Sandi lay on the mattress staring into the darkness. Overcome with the hopelessness of their miserable existence, she wept bitterly. The tears left clean streaks on her face, but could not begin to wash away the ache in her heart.

Is this all there is to life? Sandi wondered, *Can anyone help us out of this mess?*

Chapter 10

"Sandi, I have some good news for you," Mama announced happily. "I'm going to marry Lars Milliken. You girls will have a good father, and we will have a better life than we ever had before."

Sandi knew Lars. He was not like the other men Mama brought home. She could tell he liked her and the little girls and didn't give gifts simply to bribe them to stay out of the way. With all her heart, she hoped Mama was right, and life finally would get better.

Moving into the three bedroom apartment Lars had rented was a delightful experience. Sandi wandered through the spacious house, looking at all the clean, pretty rooms. There were curtains at the windows and carpets on the floors. Dared she hope it was real?

"See how excited she looks," Lars said, tilting his head toward Sandi.

"Small wonder," Mama laughed. "We've never had such a nice place to live before. This will be wonderful. Oh, Lars! I just can't believe this is happening to me."

"You've had some tough luck," Lars said tenderly, putting his arm around Mama. "But things will be different now. I'm going to give you and the girls a good life."

"And I am going to help you," Mama promised, her eyes shining with admiration and determination. "I'm going to be a real mother to my girls and a good wife to you. You'll see."

Mama kept her promise. She stopped drinking and stayed at home. She cooked regular meals, sewed clothes for the girls, and made birthday cakes. Later, Lars bought a nice house with a large backyard; and they even got a dog.

Sandi had never known life could be this good. She was deeply grateful to Lars for rescuing them from the deplorable life they had lived before. Instead of being locked in a bedroom with the little girls every night while Mama entertained strange men, they now spent evenings together as a family. Mama made supper and washed dishes while Lars mowed the lawn or watched TV. Lars' parents were Christians and took the girls into their hearts as grandchildren. At last, life was pleasant and comfortable.

During a TV commercial one evening, Lars watched Sandi sitting on the floor playing with a book of stickers.

"Sandi, where did you get those stickers?" he asked.

Sandi looked up, guilt and fear written all over her face. "At the store," she said quietly.

"Did you pay for them?" Lars asked, guessing the answer from the look on her face.

Sandi shook her head.

"Karin, come here," Lars called to Mama in the kitchen.

"Yes?" Mama asked, coming to the doorway.

"I think your daughter stole some stickers," Lars informed Mama.

"Sandi!" Mama exclaimed, snatching up the stickers. "Tell me where you got these."

Tearfully, Sandi confessed how she had slipped them inside her slacks when they were shopping.

"Did you ever take anything else?" Mama demanded.

"Some candy and little toys," Sandi sniffed.

"You little thief! You know that's stealing!" Mama grabbed Sandi by the arm and jerked her upright. "Do you want to go to jail like Skip? I'll teach you a lesson," she rushed on without waiting for an answer. Turning Sandi over her lap, Mama spanked the crying girl soundly.

"Now! Gather up all the things you stole," Mama ordered when the spanking was over. "You are going to take them back to the store and apologize. I will not have my daughter growing up to be a common criminal!"

Returning the stolen items to the store and apologizing to the manager was the most difficult thing Sandi had ever done. Although it was more unpleasant and frightening than the spanking, it was a valuable experience. There was a new sense of security in being required to do right and held accountable for her actions. All her young life she had floundered on her own, responsible only to herself.

Sandi entered third grade in yet another new school. Since this was her fourth school, and Mama had never bothered about school work, Sandi was not able to keep up with her class. With Mrs. Blackburn's help, she struggled to catch up.

"Hey, Mildew, whatcha got in the bag?" one of the boys yelled when Sandi arrived at school one morning.

"None of your business," Sandi yelled back boldly. She had no idea how she had gotten the nickname of "Mildew" at this school.

"I bet Mildew's got frog legs in her lunch," the bully called to his cronies. "Let's see."

The boys charged, and Sandi raced for the school building. She managed to beat them to the door and slipped inside to safety. Panting, she leaned against the wall to catch her breath.

"Aw, let 'er go," the bully yelled, refusing to openly admit defeat. "A one-eyed mildew girl ain't worth foolin' with."

His words slashed Sandi's spirit mercilessly. As a stranger, she had never been able to establish any friendships here. Now she thought she knew why the other children ignored or tormented her. *I'm ugly!* she thought. For the first time, she became aware how her disfigurement set her apart. How she longed to be like other children with two good, normal eyes!

She came home from school hoping to get some sympathy from Mama. But those thoughts vanished into thin air when she saw a whiskey bottle sitting on the kitchen table. "Mama! What's this?" Sandi cried out.

"Nuthin," Mama slurred. "Jus' a little somethin', fer my headache."

"But Mama!" Sandi cried again. "You said you weren't going to drink anymore."

"Now don'cha go gettin' big-mouthed on me," Mama warned menacingly. "I ain't drinkin.' I jus' needed somethin' fer a headache."

Sandi recognized that tone of voice and knew it was time to be quiet. She felt her heart sinking all the way down into her shoes, and her arms and legs suddenly lost their strength. As much as she wanted to believe it was only for a headache and Mama would not do it again, Sandi knew better. When Mama started drinking, she didn't know when to stop. The only way she could keep on living like she had been for the last year was not to drink at all.

To make matters worse, Sandi discovered Lars was drinking too. She had not known he had a drinking problem earlier. When they got married, he and Mama had agreed not to drink anymore, in order to give the girls a good home. But their pact did not last. At first Mama drank in secret, but the desire for alcohol consumed her better intentions, and she soon stopped caring who knew. Before long, she and Lars were both drinking and rapidly slipping back into the old lifestyle.

The happy months of good family life seemed like a dream to Sandi, as the old, familiar pattern of drinking and fighting returned. Once again, Sandi tried to mother the neglected, abused little girls. Mama did not cook anymore or keep the house. She and Lars argued and fought constantly.

One morning when Sandi got up for school, she found her mother gone. "Where's Mama?" Sandi asked.

"In the hospital," Lars answered strangely.

"What's wrong?" Sandi cried.

"Her jaw is broken," Lars said.

"What happened?" Sandi was aghast.

"Look," Lars explained. "I don't remember exactly what happened, but I guess I just hit her a little harder than I intended to last night. Don't worry. She can come home this morning. Her jaw will be wired shut for six weeks, but she'll be okay."

For the next six weeks Mama could eat only by drawing liquids through a straw. Never robust, she grew even thinner than before.

"I can hardly wait to sink my teeth into a hamburger," Mama said through her immobile clenched teeth as she stirred the liquid in her glass with a straw. "I am so sick of this stuff."

But when the wires were finally removed, she found the jaw muscles had grown weak from lack of use, and weeks of therapy were required before she could eat normally again.

Chapter 11

"**K**arin, we have slipped badly," Lars said one morning when they both got up with terrible hangovers. "We agreed before we were married that we would stop drinking. I don't know how we got so far so fast, but we have got to change."

"I know," Mama groaned. "But I just can't seem to help myself."

"That's the whole problem," Lars said, propping his elbows on the table and cradling his aching head in his hands. "We can't help ourselves. We need help from God."

"God?" Mama asked skeptically.

"God," Lars echoed firmly. "My parents took me to Sunday school when I was a boy. They taught me how to live right, but somehow I got on the wrong track. I need to go back to God and ask Him to help me straighten out my life."

Mama did not know what to say, so she said nothing.

"Tomorrow is Sunday. We should go to church," Lars declared.

"We?" Mama asked. "You and me, or all of us?"

"All of us," Lars clarified his statement. "I'm sure the girls would love Sunday school."

"I guess we could try it," Mama agreed slowly. "I never was a church person, but Carmen seems happier since she's going. Maybe that's what I've been looking for."

The girls loved Sunday school, just as Lars had predicted. Sylvia and Sheri were in the kindergarten class together while Sandi went with the other fourth graders. The teacher made Sandi feel welcome, and she listened intently. The story from the Bible and the songs they sang were all new to her, and she was sorry when it ended. Mama enjoyed the service more than she expected and was quite willing to attend the next Sunday.

Mama and Lars renewed their agreement to quit drinking, and life once again shifted back into a comfortable family routine. Going to church Sunday mornings became a regular part of their family life. With all her heart, Sandi hoped the change would last this time.

Sandi entered fourth grade at the same school where she had taken third grade. It was the first time in her life that she had not enrolled in a new school when the new school year began. The teacher, Mrs. Murphey, had some strange ways, and Sandi did not like her. But with a more stable home life, she was able to cope. Her grades continued to be poor, however, reflecting the turbulence of her first years at school.

When Lars bought a larger house in a nice suburb near the church they attended, he and Mama worked together, painting and getting ready to move.

On moving day Sandi sat on the edge of her bed in their new house. *A room of my own!* she exulted at the unexpected luxury. She had never had a room of her own before. *Heaven must be like this,* she thought as she looked around the lovely room.

Summer came, and Sandi relished the luxury of sleeping later in the mornings than she had been able to during school. One morning she padded softly down the carpeted hall to the kitchen for breakfast. Mama was sitting at the table with her Bible and a cup of coffee.

"Good morning, Sandi," Mama smiled, keeping her finger on the verse she had been reading. "Are the girls still sleeping?"

"Yes," Sandi answered, sliding into the chair next to Mama. "What are you reading this morning?"

In a soft voice Mama read Titus 2:11-15. Sandi snuggled against her, listening to the rise and fall of Mama's voice as she read.

"What does that mean, Mama?" Sandi asked when Mama had finished reading the passage.

"I'm not sure I understand it all myself," Mama said. "But it tells us God wants everyone to be saved. He wants us to stop doing bad things and be good. We can't be good by ourselves, so Jesus died for our sins, and He will help us be good."

"He's helping you be good, isn't He?" Sandi beamed.

"Yes," Mama hugged Sandi. "I always wanted to be a good wife and mother, but I wasn't because I drank. Drinking made me selfish. I cared more about getting a drink than I did about you. I did so many bad things."

"But you are different now," Sandi consoled Mama.

"Yes, thank God!" Mama exclaimed. "Aunt Carmen tried to tell me I needed Jesus, but I wouldn't listen. I was trying to find happiness, but looking in all the wrong places. I am going to be baptized and join the church."

"Can I do it too?" Sandi asked.

"Why—well, I don't know," Mama said uncertainly. "I don't know if the church has an age limit for baptism or not. We'll talk to the pastor about it. All right?"

Sandi nodded, satisfied the pastor could answer their question.

"What are you going to do today?" Sandi asked, slipping from her chair and going to the cupboard for a bowl of cereal.

"I thought I would make the blouse I cut yesterday for Sylvia," Mama answered. "I want you and Sylvia to have new outfits for the first day of school, and it's time to get them made. It seems *you* just started school, and now Sylvia is ready for kindergarten. My, how time flies!"

"May I make some chocolate chip cookies?" Sandi asked eagerly. "Sheri ate the last one last night."

"Sure," Mama agreed, putting her empty coffee cup on the sink. "Just be sure you clean up your mess afterward."

Sandi expertly mixed up a batch of cookies. Baking was one of the skills Mama had taught her which she thoroughly enjoyed. Humming a Sunday school song, she dropped the dough on the cookie sheet by spoonfuls.

Mama surely is a different person, Sandi mused as she slid the cookie sheet into the oven. *She is so kind and does so many nice things for us. We have lots of fun. She teaches me things, and we write poems together. She even asked me what color I thought would look best for curtains in the little girls' bedroom. I'm not afraid all the time anymore like I used to be. I hope Mama never, ever drinks again so that life stays just like this.*

Mama asked the pastor whether she and Sandi could be baptized at the same time. After questioning Sandi briefly, the pastor agreed. Although Sandi did not fully understand the Bible or the significance of baptism, she knew reading the Bible and going to church had made a great change in her mother's life. Since baptism was the right thing for a Christian, she followed her mother's example, and they were baptized together. In baptism, Sandi found a sense of security that the old lifestyle was gone and would never return.

Chapter 12

B ecause of Sandi's struggle with school work, Mrs. Murphey had wanted her to repeat fourth grade. But Mama had argued and promised to tutor Sandi and see that she caught up with the class. Under these conditions, the teacher promised to pass Sandi to fifth. Since Sandi was already behind, fifth grade work required diligent effort.

"Sandi, answer the door," Mama called from the bathroom one afternoon when the doorbell rang.

Sandi stared speechlessly at the man on the doorstep.

"Hello, Sandi. How's my little girl?" Skip's familiar voice asked.

Sandi hung onto the doorknob for support as the room spun crazily. She continued to stare and did not answer.

"Aren't you going to invite me in?" Skip asked.

Mama, hurrying around the corner, stopped and also stared in disbelief.

"Skip! What are you doing here?" Mama exclaimed.

"I came to see my little girls," Skip said defensively. "Isn't that all right?"

"Not really," Mama muttered.

"Now come on," Skip wheedled. "What's wrong with a little friendly visit with my girls?"

"Skip, I have a good husband, and we are a happy family now. I don't need you coming and spoiling things," Mama announced.

"I didn't come to spoil anything. I just came to see my girls. The courts gave me visitation rights in the divorce. I don't think you forgot I am Sylvia's natural father," Skip grinned slyly, "and you can't deny me my rights."

Mama knew Skip was right. "All right," she agreed at last.

"You may have a visit with Sylvia only, but go to McDonalds or something. I don't want you in the house."

"Fine," Skip agreed. "Bring her here."

Sylvia barely remembered Skip and went with him reluctantly. But, charmer that he was, he soon put her at ease. The visit was not the last. Slowly he broke down Mama's reserve too.

Lars was infuriated at the unwelcome appearance of this ex-husband and made no effort to hide his feelings. Mama, more attracted to Skip's tantalizing personality than she wanted to admit, defended him by pointing out he was only exercising his rights as Sylvia's natural father. The argument touched off the first real fight between

Mama and Lars since they had started going to church.

Seeing his marriage threatened by Skip's presence, Lars sought solace in a stiff drink. When Mama smelled it on his breath, all her own good intentions quickly evaporated. Lars was the one who had influenced her to go to church with him and stop drinking. If he could drink, she reasoned, so could she. One drink was all it took for her to fall headlong once again into the dizzying whirlpool of her earlier life. By the time Skip had drifted on again, she was firmly entrenched in the old pattern of drinking and violence.

When Sandi saw what was happening, she felt as if her heart had been torn out of her chest. *They had been so happy. How could Mama start drinking again?* she cried. Having held such high hopes for the future, this was a greater sorrow than ever before. Seeing all her hopes evaporate was more than she could bear.

When Sandi and Sylvia came home from school one afternoon, they could hear Mama and Lars shouting before they even got near the house.

Sandi was petrified. *This is a serious fight.* She knew the other children on the sidewalk heard the yelling, and she was terribly humiliated. Several garbage bags, ominously filled with clothes, sat on the lawn. Fear and dread ground the broken pieces of Sandi's heart into a fine powder. Packed bags of clothes could mean only one thing. They were leaving.

The girls did not want to go inside. They stood quietly by the bags, not knowing what to do.

Dragging Sheri behind her, Mama suddenly jerked open the door and slammed it shut again behind her. She was crying.

"We are leaving," Mama announced between sobs to the bewildered girls. "I am not going to put up with that man any more. I don't care if I never see him again."

"What are we going to do then?" Sandi asked.

"I'm going to call Aunt Carmen," Mama sniffled. "Come with me."

Like a row of ducklings, the three girls followed Mama to a phone booth two blocks away where she called Aunt Carmen. As she had done so many times before, Aunt Carmen came to their rescue, picking them up and then stopping by the house for the bags of clothes.

With tear-filled eyes, Sandi watched the house disappear in the distance. She was leaving behind not only the happiest time of her life, but also the only house in which she'd had a room of her own, and all her girlish treasures which Mama had neglected to pack.

Mama and the girls moved in temporarily with Aunt Carmen and Uncle Ralph. Aunt Carmen tried to reason with Mama and bring about a reconciliation between her and Lars, but Mama had made up her mind. She was finished with him forever. Instead of going back, she filed for divorce.

Feeling sorry for the girls, Aunt Carmen did all she could to make life pleasant for them. She even hauled them to school so they wouldn't have to walk. But since she lived in a different part of town, the girls had been forced to change schools again in the middle of the school year.

By the time school was over for the summer, Mama had found a two-bedroom apartment. It was only one block from the school, which would be convenient in the fall. Although the apartment was nice inside, it was a different sort of place in which to live. Having once been a store, it had big, plate glass windows in the front. Sandi liked the place all right except for the bullet hole in one of the big front windows. Even though the hole was taped shut, it was scary to think of a bullet shattering through the window into the room.

The happy family times they had known when Mama was married to Lars now faded in Sandi's memory. Had they really happened? Mama once again left the girls alone at night and made her rounds of the bars, forcing Sandi back into the role of substitute mother. Although the bottles and diapers stage was now past, Sandi faced other challenges as she took responsibility for her sisters' care and training.

"Let's clean this place today," Sandi suggested one Saturday morning. "Sylvia, you can wash the dishes, and Sheri can help me pick up things and put them away."

"I don't feel like washing dishes," Sylvia objected. "You're always making us work."

"Yeah," Sheri echoed. "What makes you think you're our boss?"

"Look, girls," Sandi pleaded. "I'm not trying to be bossy. But if we make everything nice and clean, maybe Mama will want to stay home with us tonight instead of going out."

"We tried that before, and it never works," Sylvia pointed out.

"This time we'll do an extra good job," Sandi said enthusiastically, trying to sell her plan. "I'll even wash the floor. And when we are all done, we'll find some flowers to put on the table. We can each make a card for Mama to tell her we love her. Then she will surely stay home."

"Okay," the girls agreed, catching some of Sandi's enthusiasm.

All morning the girls worked with mounting excitement and hopes that their plan would succeed. When Mama got up that afternoon, the house was as spotless as they could make it. A search of the neighborhood had yielded a handful of fresh flowers which were now in a glass of water on the kitchen table. Three cards, made from school tablet paper, were set in prominent places around the house where Mama would be sure to find them.

When Mama came out to the kitchen, she made

herself a cup of coffee and sat down at the table. She did not seem to notice the results of their day of hard work and made no comment on the clean house. She did not recognize the desperate plea for love and acceptance in the flowers and cards.

She doesn't care. It's not going to work, Sandi thought with a sinking heart as she saw her fantasy of a pleasant family evening at home evaporate.

"Where are you going?" Sandi asked as she saw Mama getting ready to leave.

"Out," Mama answered shortly. There was no need to explain, nor had there been any need for Sandi to ask the question.

"Won't you please stay home with us tonight?" Sandi pleaded.

"I have other things to do," Mama replied.

As Mama went out and shut the door, a terrible feeling of emptiness welled up within Sandi. No one seemed to realize or care how alone she was. With a desire so intense she could almost taste it, she longed for someone to care.

Night after night, after the little girls had fallen asleep, Sandi lay awake listening for Mama to come home. The knowledge that a bullet had once burst through the front window haunted her. *Suppose it happens again?* Her mind thought through possible scenarios. She tried to decide what she would do in each situation. The longer she thought about it, the more vivid the pictures in her mind became. She lay terrified until she finally heard Mama open the door and stumble inside.

Chapter 13

"**S**andi," Mama bellowed, "come here."

Sandi's stomach tied itself in a tight knot of fear and dread as she got out of bed to obey. From past experience, she was quite sure what was about to happen. Glancing at the clock as she left the room, she saw it was 2:00 a.m. Mama probably did not want anything important. She just wanted someone to yell at and beat up until the alcohol began to wear off.

"What took you so long?" Mama sneered with an oath when Sandi appeared. Her breath reeked.

"I came right away, Mama," Sandi protested.

"Don' git smart on me now, you li'le good-for-nothin' brat," Mama snarled, mingling a vicious threat with another oath. "Go down to M'Donal's and git me a hamburger."

"Now?" Sandi asked in astonishment.

"Tha's what I said, didn't I?" Mama snapped. "An' be quick abou' it!"

Mama often came home, ranting and raving, at this hour of the morning. She would scold and push the girls around for reasons her imagination manufactured. Sandi knew better than to argue with her now over this ridiculous demand, even though she knew by the time she returned with the hamburger Mama would probably have changed her mind and not even eat it. Such things had happened before.

Sandi went to Mama's room to hunt for some money while Mama went into the bathroom. There was a moan and the terrible sound of retching, followed by a thump. It had occurred before. Just as Sandi expected, Mama had passed out and lay on the floor where she had vomited.

Holding her breath, Sandi grasped Mama under the arms and dragged her out of her own filth.

"Sandi, I'm sick," Mama moaned as she started to regain consciousness. "Help me get to bed."

Sandi half carried, half dragged Mama to her room where she stripped off her filthy clothes and helped her get into bed. Sobbing softly, Sandi got a bucket of water and began the loathsome task of cleaning the bathroom floor as she had so many times before.

Oh God! her heart cried as she knelt on the floor with the rag in her hand, *Why do we have to live like this? Nobody loves us. Nobody cares about us. Is it my fault? Did I do something wrong? God, what shall I do? How can we get out of this mess?* She was too distraught to listen for an answer.

In the morning, Sandi dragged herself out of bed. Lying awake every night, waiting for Mama to come in and then caring for her, robbed Sandi of needed sleep. Yet, it was her responsibility to see that she and her sisters got to school on time in the morning.

The next day, the sixth grade history book swam before Sandi's face as she tried to study. She was too tired to concentrate on the words. Added to the mind-numbing weariness were the memories of last night and a dread of tonight. Knowing her family was not like other families was humiliating to Sandi. With these thoughts occupying her mind, there was little room for history or any other subject. Trying to study at home was useless, for then she was busy caring for her sisters and running the household.

Mama often played on the sympathies of others, portraying herself as a victim of circumstances beyond her control. "Down on my luck," she would say. While Sandi was glad for gifts of food, clothing, and toys, she also felt sorry for these generous people, because Mama was taking advantage of them.

Mama also got food stamps, but she turned over the grocery shopping to Sandi, who found a sense of fulfillment in this responsibility and in cooking.

"Girls, I have to go for groceries," Sandi told her younger sisters one afternoon when they got home from school. "You stay in the house until I get back. And don't let any men in."

To get to the Safeway where she shopped, Sandi

had to ride four blocks and cross a four-lane highway. Although she could easily have walked that distance, she always took her bike for security, thinking she had a better chance to escape if any men tried to stop her.

The trip to Safeway was uneventful, and Sandi walked up and down the aisles choosing whatever looked good to eat. Before she realized it, the grocery cart was nearly filled. Knowing she could not transport so much on her bike, she regretfully returned a package of cookies and a few other items to the shelves and headed for the checkout.

After paying for the groceries with Mama's food stamps, Sandi carried her groceries out to her bike. She put one bag in the basket attached to the handlebars, set another on the seat, and squeezed the third between the basket and handlebars. Setting out slowly, she tried to balance everything as she pushed the bike along.

After waiting for a break in the traffic, Sandi pushed the bike out onto the highway. Her heart pounded in fear as she wheeled the bike across the first two lanes. She gave the bike an extra thrust so it would hop up over the curb onto the median strip. Unfortunately, this caused the bag on the handlebars to fall off. It split open, spilling its contents over the road.

Sandi set the other two bags of groceries on the grassy median strip and scurried about, collecting spilled groceries while approaching cars swung around her. With her heart pounding from fear, embarrassment, and exertion, she retreated to the safety of the median strip.

What shall I do? Sandi's mind raced, considering her predicament. *I need another bag for this stuff. But if I leave it and go back to the store, somebody might steal it. They might take my bike too.*

Cars whizzed by frighteningly near. The thought of someone stopping frightened her too. She had learned not to trust strangers, no matter how friendly they seemed, or how desperate her situation. A huge lump rose in her throat, and hot tears burned her eyes. Crying would not help, but she was at her wit's end.

One of the baggers in the store had been amused when he saw the pre-teen girl loading three bags of groceries onto her bike. Knowing the risk she was taking, he had watched her cross the road and had witnessed the disaster at the median strip. Taking several bags with him, he crossed the street and approached the stricken girl.

Sandi saw him coming, and even though she knew he was from Safeway, she was afraid because she feared all men. He did not say a word, but silently helped repack her groceries into new bags. Then he carefully reloaded the bike and pushed it across the other two lanes of the highway.

"Thank you!" Sandi said with a sigh of relief.

"You'll be all right now," the man said kindly as he turned to go back to Safeway.

Sandi slowly pushed the bike the four blocks home. Her heart, warmed and encouraged by her rescue from a hopeless situation, overflowed with gratitude. The kind man's simple act of consideration beamed like a bright light of love in her dark life of abuse and neglect.

Life had become a series of traumatic experiences and constant turmoil. Mama was always angry with the girls or fighting with her boyfriends and sisters. Desperate to change things, Sandi began calling the bars Mama frequented to find out where she was. Somehow, she hoped it would make Mama think about the girls and come home earlier. The worst part of being alone at night was knowing Mama was giving the attention that belonged to her daughters to a succession of strange men, leaving her children betrayed and utterly forsaken.

When the girls returned home from school in the afternoon, Mama was usually out of bed, getting ready to go out for the night. One afternoon, the house seemed strangely quiet and empty. Sandi's quick search ended in Mama's bedroom where she lay still in bed, asleep. Something peculiar about her color and breathing alarmed Sandi.

"Mama," Sandi called urgently, "wake up." There was no answer. "Mama! Wake up!" Sandi called again, louder this time. She shook her mother's shoulder, but there was still no response of any kind.

I've got to get help! Sandi thought wildly. *Mama must have overdosed on drugs. She will die unless we get her to the hospital—FAST!*

Running to the telephone, Sandi dialed Mama's current boyfriend, Tom, and was relieved to hear him answer. Rapidly, she spilled the problem. He promised to come at once.

In minutes, Tom arrived and strode to Mama's bedroom. He quickly sized up the situation.

"Get her dressed," Tom ordered Sandi, "and then I'll take her to the hospital."

Mama was sleeping so deeply she did not make a sound. She flopped unresponsively when Sandi turned her on her side to dress her.

"I'll take this side and you take that side," Tom instructed Sandi. "We'll carry her out to my truck. I guess we'll have to lay her in the back."

Carrying a blanket and pillow for Mama, terrified Sylvia and Sheri brought up the rear of the bizarre procession. They all crowded in the front after positioning Mama as comfortably as possible in the back.

Soon Tom was backing up to the emergency entrance of the hospital. "I think she tried to kill herself," he told the attendant.

The doctors and nurses sprang into action. Mama was loaded onto a litter and rushed into a treatment room. Finding seats in the waiting room, the three frightened girls sat stiffly in a row with Tom. They could hear the sounds of their mother's stomach being pumped in the next room. They did not know how long ago or on what drugs she had overdosed.

"Oh, God!" Sandi poured out the agony of her terrified heart to the only One who could help them. "Why did this have to happen? Will life always be like this? Why can't things get better? We may already be too late. What will happen to us if Mama dies? God, help us! I don't know what to do."

"I think we got her just in time," the doctor reported. "She will probably remain asleep until morning. We'll keep her here until we're sure she is all right."

When Mama woke up, she was disappointed to find she was still alive. "Why didn't you let me die?" she cried angrily. "Life isn't worth living. I want to die and get out of this misery."

"You need to ask God to help you, Mama," Sandi tried to counsel her mother.

"God?!" Mama mocked weakly. "He can't be bothered with the likes of me. I'm a hopeless case."

Chapter 14

Though thoroughly disillusioned with her life, Mama returned to her old lifestyle and nothing changed. She continued seeking elusive happiness by pursuing the same things that had failed her before.

"I'm getting married again," Mama announced abruptly to the girls. "His name is Wade Richart. He's a widower with two children. Max is twelve—Sandi's age, and Marie is ten."

Sandi groaned. In addition to adjusting to a new stepfather, this time they would also have to learn to live with a new stepbrother and sister.

Wade was an alcoholic like Mama's three previous husbands. The drinking and fighting in the home continued without letup, and conditions worsened drastically. Like Mama, Wade turned violent with alcohol. Both of them abused the children without reason, whipping them severely enough to cause deep purple bruises. The emotional pain that accompanied the undeserved beatings went even deeper than the visible bruises.

When school opened in September, the children felt relieved to escape the harsh home atmosphere for at least the length of a school day. Since Sandi was beginning seventh grade, she had to change schools again to attend junior high school. Entering a different school on the opening day was almost routine by now. This was the fifth school she had attended so far.

One of the differences between junior high and elementary school, Sandi soon learned, was the absence of daily recesses. Instead, one class period each week was set aside for gym class. The girls were required to play in shorts and take showers afterwards.

Gym class was a welcome break from studying all day, and Sandi looked forward to it. But one day, after a particularly severe belting the night before, she found herself dreading gym class as much as she had welcomed it before.

What shall I do? Sandi asked herself in sudden panic. *I can't wear gym shorts. Everyone will see the bruises on my legs.*

Taking an easy way out, Sandi made up a plausible excuse and was allowed to wear her slacks. But by the next week, new bruises had been added to the old ones, which were now a sickening yellow color. The excuse Sandi had used the week before had worked so well she tried it again.

"Sandi, that excuse is worn out," the gym teacher said when Sandi gave it the third week.

"What is the real reason you don't want to wear shorts?"

Sandi hung her head. "I can't tell you," she mumbled.

"I think you should see the guidance counselor," the gym teacher said. "I'll call and tell her you're coming."

Sandi walked down the long hall to the counselor's office. This was not a punishment, but it was humiliating, because a trip to the guidance counselor showed a person was having a problem. Mrs. Kelly was a kind, sympathetic person whom students trusted. They knew they could confide in her, and she would do her best to help find solutions to their problems.

Kindly, gently, Mrs. Kelly drew out Sandi's reason for refusing to wear shorts for gym class.

"I am going to call the school nurse," Mrs. Kelly said when she saw the bruises on Sandi's legs. "I'd like her to see this and help us decide what to do about it."

"Do you have any brothers or sisters?" the school nurse asked after examining Sandi's bruises.

Sandi gave the names and ages of her sisters, as well as those of her stepbrother and sister. The nurse examined all four of them. When she found the same kind of bruises on them all, she called the police. All five children were taken into police custody, and child abuse charges were filed against

Mama and Wade.

"We have found homes for all of you," the guidance counselor told the frightened group huddled in her office. "Sylvia and Sheri will be going to a home here in the city. Sandi, Max, and Marie will be going to another home in the country. They are both good homes and I think you will like them."

"How long will we have to stay?" Sandi asked the question uppermost in each of the children's minds.

"I don't know for sure," Mrs. Kelly answered. "That depends on several things. But it will not be permanent. We will try to get you back to your parents as soon as we can."

When she had confided in the guidance counselor, Sandi had never imagined such drastic measures would be taken. The chain of events occurred with dizzying speed, and before she knew it, she was in a car with Max and Marie on her way to a horse farm in the country.

If Sandi had not been so distraught at the sudden turn of events, she would have been awed at the sight of the home to which she was taken. The spacious lawn and pastures were surrounded by white board fences. The house sat on a little rise like a jewel on a crown. As they drove up the long sloping drive, she could have felt fortunate. But separated from her sisters for the first time in her life, she felt utterly alone and hopeless.

Chapter 15

Sandi, Marie, and Max got out of the car and slowly followed the caseworker to the door. A friendly woman warmly invited them all inside.

"This is Judy Morris," the caseworker told the children. "She will be your foster mother, and I'm sure you will like her."

During the introductions, two girls slipped into the room to inspect the new arrivals. Sandi stared at them curiously, unaware she was doing so. The older girl was beautiful and tastefully dressed. She carried a refined air of elegance and sophistication. Sandi guessed the younger girl, who looked more carefree and lively, to be about her own age.

"I will let you introduce your daughters," the caseworker told Mrs. Morris.

"This is Shirlyn," Mrs. Morris said, gesturing toward the older girl. "She is sixteen, and Dedra is twelve," she motioned toward the younger one.

The children acknowledged the introductions stiffly, each group sizing up the other. As the caseworker and Mrs. Morris concluded their business,

Sandi glanced around the room. Although the house would not qualify as wealthy, it certainly had a comfortable, homey look.

When the caseworker left, Mrs. Morris showed the children to their rooms. Max would use the room which had belonged to an older son. Sandi and Marie would share a bedroom.

"I hope you will feel at home with us," Mrs. Morris smiled, giving Sandi a quick hug. "We aren't rich, but we're happy to share what we have. I'm sure this has been a tough day for you. We'll try to get you to bed early tonight so that you'll be ready to go to school tomorrow morning. Our children ride the bus, but I'll take you in myself tomorrow to get you registered and settled in."

Max loved living on the farm. Whenever he was not in school, he shadowed Mr. Morris and adjusted rapidly to the change. Marie followed his lead and accepted the situation. But Sandi, homesick for her sisters, found it impossible to enjoy what could have been a pleasant experience. Shirlyn and Dedra, even though they treated her well, could not replace her own sisters. Being in high school, Shirlyn had a circle of friends and activities separate from the younger girls. Dedra, the baby of the family, was spoiled. She was not unkind to her foster sisters, but neither did she try to include them in her life.

In spite of Mrs. Morris' attempts to make the

children feel at home, Sandi felt like an outcast. Night after night, she cried herself to sleep with homesickness for her sisters. In vivid nightmares she saw them or Mama being hurt in fights, falling down stairs, or dying. Her terrified shrieks often shattered the silence of the night.

"Sandi, Sandi," Mrs. Morris soothed, cradling the screaming girl in her arms. "Wake up. It's all right. You're safe here in your bed."

Sandi clung savagely to her foster mother. Her shrieks changed to wild weeping and finally dissolved into quiet sobs as Mrs. Morris continued to hold her and stroke her forehead, speaking comforting words. Slowly Sandi realized it had only been a dream, and Mama was not dead.

Mrs. Morris was not unduly alarmed the first time Sandi had a nightmare. She assumed it was part of getting adjusted to the new home. But when the nightmares continued night after night, and sometimes more than once a night, Mrs. Morris spoke to a caseworker who made an appointment for Sandi with a psychologist.

Left alone with Mrs. Williams, the psychologist, Sandi was thoroughly frightened. Depending on the outcome, she could be determined mentally unbalanced and even institutionalized. Desperately pleading her case, Sandi poured out her story, neither embroidering the facts nor hiding anything. She shared the fears resulting from years of physical and mental abuse, and the turmoil, neglect, and rejection that had been her life for most of her twelve years.

"I really don't think there is anything wrong with me," Sandi concluded passionately when she had finished her story. "If you had been through what I've been through, you would have nightmares too."

Mrs. Williams sat silently, looking back over the notes she had taken as Sandi spoke. When she looked up, her eyes showed only compassion for the young girl before her.

"You're right," Mrs. Williams agreed, after asking a few more questions. "I think nightmares are not abnormal for someone with the hard times you have had."

Sandi's relief was obvious. "Thank you, Mrs. Williams," she breathed through a rainbow smile. She could not put into words how unnerving it was to think she might be diagnosed with a mental problem.

"You may be excused," Mrs. Williams said. "I want to speak with your caseworker for a few minutes. I will report my findings to her. In time, I'm sure you will be fine."

While the children were in foster homes, Mama and Wade appeared in court several times and were required to take family counseling. After several months, they managed to convince the authorities they were responsible parents, and the children were all returned to them.

As soon as Sandi returned home, Mama launched into a long tirade, blaming her for the whole episode, since she had talked with the guidance counselor. The longer Mama talked, the more blame she heaped upon Sandi's young shoulders, including blame for Mama's failed marriages and everything else that had gone wrong in her life.

"You make me sick," Mama shrieked. "I can't stand the sight of you. You can just go live with your dad."

Sandi was terrified. Surely Mama would not send her to live with Norman Hackman! Sandi had heard many stories about the bad things he had done. Living in his house would surely be awful. But, with Mama so bitter against her, she knew there was a very real possibility she would be sent to live with him.

Sandi lived in daily terror, trying to please Mama every way she could, but it was no use. Nothing pleased Mama.

"I've had it!" Mama shouted several days later in a fit of anger. "You're going."

Marching directly to the phone, Mama called Norman.

"Like it or not," she snapped, "Sandi is coming to live with you. You're her father, and I'm not tolerating her here a minute longer."

Norman gave his consent, and Sandi promptly found herself on a bus heading to yet another life and home.

Chapter 16

Sandi searched the depot waiting room when she stepped off the bus in her dad's town. She did not remember her father or have any idea how she would recognize him. He had not seen her since she was a toddler. But she and her father looked so much alike that they recognized each other instantly.

With her heart in her throat, Sandi apprehensively scrutinized the man in western clothes and cowboy boots coming towards her. This was the man about whom Mama had told her such terrible stories. He was only average height, but solidly built. He wasn't extremely overweight, but his stomach bulged out above his belt. He looked ordinary enough, but she knew appearances could be deceiving.

The man stopped in front of her and stammered, "S-S-Sandi Hackman?"

"Yes," Sandi answered faintly as she looked up.

"And I'm your dad," the big man boomed as he slid his strong arm around her shoulder and hugged her. "It's b-b-been a long time since I saw my little girl. I'm g-g-g-lad to have you back."

Sandi smiled up at him dubiously. Her apprehensions melted a little with this warm welcome, but she had learned not to trust anyone too soon, especially not men. Time would tell what kind of person he really was.

"You c-c-came at a good time," Dad said when Sandi's baggage had been stowed in the back of the pickup, and they were headed toward his house. "Dottie, that's my wife, just left with the kids y-y-yesterday and went to her parents for a week of vacation. We have a whole w-w-week to ourselves to learn to know each other again. We'll have a great time. Wh-wh-what would you like to do?"

"I don't know," Sandi faltered. "Whatever you want to do." She had no idea what he liked to do or what he considered "a great time" to be.

"H-H-How about a ball game?" Dad suggested. "The St. Louis Cardinals are p-p-playing the Kansas City Royals. Would you like to go s-s-see the game?"

"Sure," Sandi agreed, warming a little to this man with the habitual stammer. She had never been to a big league game, and it sounded exciting.

Dad found seats for them when they got to the stadium. Although he preferred beer for himself, he kept Sandi supplied with hot dogs and cokes. They shouted themselves hoarse, rooting for the Royals. By the time the game was over, Sandi felt she and Dad were becoming good friends. He did not seem to be at all like Mama had said he was.

Dad was as good as his word, and the ball game was only the beginning of a great week. Every day he had a new plan for something to do together. By the end of the week her fear of him had dissolved completely, and they were on perfectly friendly terms. She told him about Mama and her sisters, and he told her about his absent family. Dottie was a lab technician who worked at the local hospital. Their son Eric was seven, and Connie was five.

Sandi felt special, knowing Dad had taken the week off from his truck driving job just to spend time with her. She could tell he loved her and was trying, as best he could, to compensate for the years of hardship she had endured with Mama.

Mama lied about Dad, Sandi decided. *She did me a favor by sending me to live with him. I know he is my REAL father because we look so much alike. I think I have finally found a place where I am wanted and belong. I hope I can always live here.*

Just as Sandi finished washing the dishes one evening, a car pulled into the drive.

"H-H-Here comes Dottie and the kids," Dad said.

Sandi could not miss the anxious tone in his voice. Her own anxiety mounted as she watched while the unattractive, very overweight woman and two children spilled out of the car and began to unload the trunk.

Eric and Connie followed their mother to the house, quarreling as they came. Dottie opened the door and heaved her suitcase inside. Turning her back to the room, she settled the children's argument before coming inside. Puffing, she bent to retrieve the handle of her suitcase, but pulled herself up sharply as she caught sight of Sandi standing beside her father.

"Dottie, this is my daughter, S-S-Sandi," Dad said before Dottie could say a word. "She c-c-came to live with us."

Dottie stared in shock and disbelief at the girl in her kitchen. Hostility and resentment flashed across her face. Sandi cringed, her spirit shriveling under Dottie's piercing glare.

"S-S-Sandi is from my first marriage," Dad hastened to explain. "Her mother s-s-sent her to me."

"Well!" Dottie spat at Dad. "You sure like to pull surprises, don't you?"

"I ca-ca-can't refuse my own daughter a home," Dad said weakly.

"She can stay; only it would have been nice to have been informed," Dottie assented sarcastically.

The pleasant life with Dad was over. Everything changed the minute his wife stepped in the door and saw Sandi. The next morning, Dad left on the truck and did not come home again for nearly two weeks, leaving Sandi to try to fit herself into a family where she was clearly not welcome.

Dottie knew Norman was unfaithful while he was on the road, and Sandi's presence in the home was a constant reminder to her of other women in his life. When Norman was not trucking, he spent most of his time at bars, where Dottie regularly collected him, forcing him home. Although they fought constantly, she stayed with him because she felt she would not be able to get any other husband.

Although Dottie did not physically abuse Sandi, the verbal and emotional abuse was extremely painful.

"Oh, no! You sit in the back seat," Dottie commanded sharply when Sandi reached for the front car door handle.

Eric and Connie sat in the front with their mother as they rode to church, making Sandi keenly aware that she was excess baggage in their lives.

When they got out of the car at church and started toward the door, Dottie hissed, "You walk behind us."

Humiliated, Sandi trailed her stepfamily into the church. This was the method Dottie used to constantly remind Sandi she did not belong with them. Eric and Connie got the best and first choice of everything, while Sandi had to be content with second place or whatever was left.

When Sandi started eighth grade at still another school, she once again lagged behind the rest of the class.

"How can you be so stupid?" Dottie belittled Sandi. She didn't know or consider how attending seven schools in eight years had affected Sandi's ability to learn.

Dad was very nice to Sandi when he was home. But that was not very often or very long at a time. He bought her a bike and gave her a nice camera for her birthday. Although he was always kind to her himself, he could not have helped seeing how unfairly Dottie treated his daughter.

Why doesn't Dad do something to help me? Sandi wondered. *I know he sees how Dottie treats me, but he won't make her stop. I guess he would rather let her mistreat me than fight with her over it. He doesn't have any backbone. I don't like it here after all. I wish I could go home, but I can't. Mama doesn't want me anymore.*

More than once, Sandi cried herself to sleep, lonely for Mama and her sisters. Even though life with Mama was hard, there was a bond between them that did not exist with Dad and his family.

Maybe it will get better after a while, Sandi kept telling herself. *Give them some time. Maybe they will get used to me. Give it a year. Wait it out and see if it gets better.*

After a year went by without any improvement, Sandi gave up hoping. *I can't take this any longer,* she decided. *I'll run away and go back to Mama.* She would rather take life with Mama as it was than continue to live here as an unwelcome foreigner.

Secretly, Sandi thought out her plan of escape. She had no money for a bus ticket, nor could she ask for any. Somehow she would have to rely on her own wits to get home to Mama. Although it was a long way to ride on a bike, she thought she could do it. Over and over, she mentally mapped out the best route to take. She would take back roads as much as possible to avoid being picked up by police, or being seen by anyone who might suspect what she was doing. She did not know when the opportunity would come, but while she waited, she prepared for it the best she could.

Chapter 17

"**G**randpas are here," Connie sang out when she saw Grandpa Hackman's car turn into the driveway one Sunday.

"You go out and find something to do," Dottie snapped in a fierce undertone to Sandi as Grandpa Hackmans approached the door. "We don't need you hanging around while we talk."

Sandi understood. Learning to know her Hackman relatives had been one of the benefits of the year with Dad. Grandpa and Grandma Hackman were glad to have her in the family, but Dottie tried to keep them apart as much as possible, without being openly rude to Grandpas. She was afraid Sandi would tell them how she was being treated.

"All right," Sandi readily agreed, grabbing her hood sweater. "Hi, Grandma and Grandpa," she said brightly as they met at the door. "I was just leaving to ride over to my friend's house. Hope you don't mind."

"No. That's fine," Grandma smiled.

"See you later," Sandi called and waved as she

walked to the garage for her bike.

She said, "Find something to do," Sandi thought fiercely. *All right, I'll find something to do. This is my chance to run away.*

With the blood pounding in her ears, Sandi wheeled her bike out of the garage. Hopping on, she headed down the driveway. *I wish I could take some of my things with me,* she thought sadly. *I can always get other clothes, but I hate to leave my beads and the camera Dad gave me. But there's no way I can take anything without Dottie getting suspicious. I have to get a good start before they miss me.*

Taking the back road as she had planned earlier, Sandi pedaled as fast as she could to cover the 20 miles home. Mile after mile, fear chased her until she was hot and panting in spite of the cool weather. She was afraid that when her grandparents and Dottie realized she had run away, they would send the police to find her and bring her back. The 20 miles seemed like 40 to her.

Puffing from exertion, Sandi found it impossible to pedal up the steep hill that rose before her. She got off the bike and pushed it up the gravel road. She badly needed to rest, but fear drove her on.

Just then a car came tearing over the top of the hill toward her. Stones flew as the driver braked. Now a new fear seized her. *Strangers! Bad men! What if they try to pick me up?*

Sandi leaped on the bike and struggled to pedal

up the steep hill. She heard the car stop and back up. *I've got to get away before they hurt me!* she thought wildly.

"Sandi!" a familiar voice called from the car. "Sandi!"

Sandi turned and nearly fell off the bike from the sudden weak relief that flooded her. It was Kirby, one of her Gilmore cousins.

"What are you doing way out here?" Kirby asked curiously.

Sandi wheeled her bike over to the car. "I'm running away," she gasped.

"Running away?" Kirby asked in astonishment. "What for?"

"I just can't take the way Dottie treats me anymore," Sandi explained. "She puts on a nice front, but she treats me like dirt at home. I'm sick of it so I'm running away."

"Where are you going?" Kirby asked.

"Back to Mama," Sandi said, not mentioning that she was unsure of her welcome.

"You've got a ways to go yet," Kirby observed.

"I know," Sandi admitted. "But I can do it before dark."

"I can drop you off at Grandpas on my way home," Kirby offered. "It would save you a lot of time and miles."

"You're sure you don't mind?" Sandi hesitated.

"Not at all," Kirby reassured her. "We can put your bike in the trunk."

"I'll take you up on it. Thanks," Sandi accepted the offer gratefully.

The remaining few miles melted rapidly away as the car sped down the road. Sandi sank back in the seat, thankful for the rest. She would be forever grateful to this cousin for helping her escape her stepmother.

When they arrived at Grandpa Gilmores, no one answered the doorbell. The house was silent and empty.

"There's nobody home," Sandi's voice betrayed her disappointment. "But I guess they'll soon come. You can go. Thanks for bringing me."

"I'm not going to leave you here on the doorstep," Kirby protested. "I'll take you to Aunt Tina. Her house isn't far from here. Hop in."

Sandi was relieved to find Aunt Tina at home, and Tina was more than willing to help when she heard her niece's problems.

"Grandpas are down at their cabin on the lake with Aunt Carmen and Uncle Ralph," Aunt Tina said. "I'll call them."

His mission accomplished, Kirby unloaded Sandi's bike and left while Aunt Tina made the call. "Good luck," he called to Sandi as he backed out of the drive.

"Thanks," Sandi called back. "Thanks so much for helping me."

Aunt Carmen was as surprised as Aunt Tina when she heard of Sandi's sudden, unannounced appearance. But she promised to come and pick her up.

On the way back to the cabin, Aunt Carmen listened sympathetically to Sandi's story of life at her father's house and why she had run away.

"So I just got sick of it and came back to Mama," Sandi finished. "Is she at the cabin with you and Grandpas?"

"No," Aunt Carmen hesitated momentarily. Then swiftly deciding Sandi may as well know the truth right away, she added, "She took Sylvia and Sheri and went back to California about six months ago."

"Oh!" Sandi almost choked as tears came to her eyes. The realization that she had been left behind stabbed a deep gash in her heart. All the hopes she had built of a better life with Mama came crashing to the ground. Mama had left without a word. There was no home here for her after all.

"Don't send me back to Dad," Sandi pleaded. "I'll do anything just so I don't have to go back."

"We'll talk to Grandpa about it," Aunt Carmen promised, "and see what he thinks we should do."

"We'll call your mother and see if she'll take you back again," Grandpa decided. "If she says you can come back, I'll buy you a plane ticket."

No one knew whether Mama was still angry with Sandi or how she would react to the news that Sandi wanted to return. Sandi was so desperate to keep from being sent back to Dad, she decided to tell Mama Dad was guilty of incest. She knew it was wrong to tell such a lie, but she thought that was the story most likely to convince Mama to take her back.

Mama listened to Sandi's apology for the problems that had divided them a year ago and the made-up story of her father's abuse.

"If Grandpa is willing to buy you a ticket, you may come," Mama said, accepting Sandi's apology without comment.

"She said I can come," Sandi laughed in weak relief as she hung up the phone. "I guess she got over being mad at me."

"Then we better go home and get you ready to leave," Grandpa said.

Since Sandi had no luggage, Grandma packed some of the things Mama had left behind. The next morning Grandpa and Grandma took her to the airport and saw her off to California.

As the plane taxied down the runway and lifted off into the sky, Sandi finally relaxed. Now she had truly escaped from Dottie. Surely by now they had missed Sandi, and figured she had run away, but no one had come looking for her. Now that she could think about it without fear, she doubted Dottie even cared she was gone. Her stepmother was probably glad just to be rid of her.

Chapter 18

S andi scanned the people waiting to meet passengers at the airport gate. *There she is! And Skip's mother too.* Sandi waved, and Mama waved back. Her smile reassured Sandi. *She was welcome!* And in a minute they were hugging each other.

"Where are Sylvia and Sheri?" Sandi asked, releasing Mama and stepping back.

"They weren't home from school yet," Mama said. "But they should be by now. They are really excited about you coming home."

"I'm glad to be back together too," Sandi acknowledged. "I *never* want to live with Dad again. I didn't like Dottie."

"She didn't seem like a very pleasant person when I talked to her," Mama agreed.

"When did you talk to her?" Sandi asked in amazement.

"I tried to call you a couple of times, but she wouldn't let me talk to you," Mama said. "You never answered my letters, so I thought you didn't want anything to do with me anymore."

"I never got any letters from you. Dottie must have thrown them away!" Sandi gasped. Knowing Mama had not totally abandoned her was a comforting relief.

Mama ground her cigarette into the sand of a nearby ashtray and swore. Changing the subject, she said, "Let's get your bags."

After claiming their baggage, they headed for home. Sandi was surprised to learn that home was a camper. Stepgrandma had moved there after losing the lease on her house, and Mama had "temporarily" moved in with her when she came to California.

Living at the campground was unique. Made to sleep five, the camper was quite crowded with Sandi's arrival. It was parked adjacent to the public bathroom, and they washed their dishes in a basin outside. Mama intended to move into an apartment as soon as possible, but she couldn't afford it yet. Sylvia, past her tenth birthday, and Sheri, now nine, had both grown since Sandi had last seen them.

"Mama and Wade got divorced," Sylvia explained, bringing Sandi up to date. "Mama decided to come out here and see whether she could get back with Skip again, but it didn't work out. So we moved in here with my grandma, and Mama got a job."

"What does she do?" Sandi asked.

Sylvia made a face. "She's a dancer in a bar."

"I wish I hadn't asked," Sandi groaned.

"At least, living here in this camper, she doesn't bring men home," Sylvia pointed out.

"That's one plus," Sandi agreed.

"She had an abortion a couple months ago," Sylvia said. "We didn't find out until later. We thought she just had the flu or something until Grandma told us what really happened."

"Looks like not much has changed," Sandi remarked.

"Mama will never change," Sylvia laughed bitterly.

"We can always hope," Sandi suggested.

"Well, it's not too bad right now," Sylvia shrugged. "I kind of like living here. Just so the men stay away."

But Mama was the kind who always thought she needed a man. And her job provided plenty of opportunities for meeting them. When she brought José Perez home, the girls instinctively knew he was not a desirable person. He was short and fat, had a stiff, black mustache, and soon proved to be rude and grouchy. Stepgrandma did not like having him around either. She tried to make Mama see he was not the kind of man she needed, but Mama would not listen.

"For the life of me, I don't see what you want with that José," Stepgrandma grumbled. "If you insist on bringing him around, you'll have to move out. I don't want him around."

"All right," Mama snapped. "We'll move out then, and you can have your camper to yourself."

It was no idle threat. Mama rented another camper in the same campground and moved herself and the girls into it. José moved in with them.

The girls had not liked José before, and living with him only intensified their feelings. Although he drank constantly, he did not need alcohol to make him mean. He was ill-tempered and mean by nature. He bullied the girls, found fault with the things they did, and blamed them for things they did not do. He made up excuses to hit them, and found a bizarre satisfaction in tormenting them.

"This dish is not clean," José yelled, waking the girls after they had gone to bed for the night. "Get up and wash them all over again."

"I'm not gonna do that," Sandi yelled back. "You aren't my boss."

"Oh, yeah," José lunged and grabbed her. "I'll teach you not to smart-mouth me," he bellowed a Spanish oath as he slapped her repeatedly across the face.

Life was a series of such battles. Sandi hated the way she argued and fought with José, but she wasn't about to accept the undeserved treatment. Because she opposed him most, she was hit most often. Mama was well aware of the way he treated the girls, but did nothing to stop it.

Why doesn't Mama put us first? Sandi thought angrily. *Why is this stupid guy she met in a bar more important than her own daughters? Why can't she see her daughters' love is more valuable than the favors of this mean man she picked up along the way? Why doesn't she defend us when he picks on us?*

In their own way, the girls got even with José by taking the change out of his pants pockets while he slept. They kept the money hidden in a jar until it was filled and then treated themselves to movies or bought things to eat.

One day as Sandi was passing the soda machine, she saw Corey, the neighbor boy, reaching up into the slot of the machine with his fingers.

"What are you doing?" Sandi asked curiously.

Corey jumped. "Oh, it's you," he laughed when he saw her. "Watch this." He stuck his fingers in the machine again, and a quarter popped out of the slot.

"Hey, neat!" Sandi exclaimed. "How did you do that?"

Corey showed her how it was done, and soon she could flip quarters out of the machine as fast as he could. Quarters added up fast, and the value of the hidden money jar spiraled upward rapidly. Sandi took her sisters on a shopping excursion, buying clothes and food. Being able to buy things for them made her feel important.

The girls discovered another bonanza in the trash barrels around the campground. They were amazed how many good things people threw away.

113

One Saturday morning as the girls were making their usual weekly round of the trash barrels, they met an unfamiliar lady.

"Good morning, girls," the lady smiled.

"Good morning," the girls answered, hiding their trash can treasures behind their backs.

"My name is Juanita. What are your names?" the lady asked.

"I'm Sandi, and this is Sylvia, and Sheri," Sandi answered, speaking for them all.

"Do you live here?" Juanita asked.

"Yes," Sandi answered.

"I am from the Nazarene church," Juanita began to explain her mission in the campground. "Our church is running a bus to pick up children who would like to go to Sunday school. We will be stopping here on Sunday morning. We would love to have you girls come along. Do you go to church somewhere?"

"No," Sandi answered. "We used to go to church, but we don't anymore."

"Would you like to?" Juanita asked.

"Yes. I would," Sandi nodded. "Mama wouldn't care."

"Be at the front entrance at nine o'clock Sunday morning then." Juanita smiled a warm welcome. "The bus will be there. And I'll be looking for all three of you at church."

"Okay," Sandi promised.

"She looked like a nice lady," Sylvia commented

114

when Juanita had walked away.

"Yeah, and she sure smelled good too," Sheri added.

Sandi had also been impressed with Juanita. Although Mama had long ago dropped the habit of going to church, the girls had sporadically attended various churches as they moved from place to place. But now Sandi suddenly knew she wanted to be on that morning Sunday school bus more than anything else in the world.

The next morning, the three sisters were at the designated place and rode the bus to the Nazarene church. Sandi was not sure which she wanted more—to be in church or to see Juanita again. There was something magnetic about her that Sandi could not explain. Somehow, she sensed Juanita could help fill an empty spot in their love-starved lives.

Juanita seemed to understand the longing in the girls she had found digging through trash barrels. Moved with compassion for these mistreated girls, she spent time with them, baking cookies at her house, shopping, or helping them with their homework. Sandi would have been lost in her first year of high school without Juanita's help.

By her life, Juanita showed the difference Christ makes in a person. The girls found her home a calm, quiet haven from the turbulence of their own. Juanita radiated the love of Christ in the gentle, sweet way she spoke and moved about.

More than anything, Sandi wanted to be like her, but Sandi's actual performance fell miserably short of her ideal. *I would like so badly to be like her, but I know I never can.*

Although Sandi had been baptized when she was ten years old and assumed she was a Christian, she had not really understood the doctrines of sin and salvation. Now for the first time, she began to understand her personal responsibility for sin and God's gift of salvation through faith in Jesus.

Late one night after everyone was asleep, Sandi sat looking out through the little camper window at the stars. She cried out to her Maker, "Oh God! Why is my life like this? Why is our home always filled with anger and fighting? Is it really my fault Mama's life is so miserable? I don't want to be like Mama and drink and do drugs. Please help me. Sometimes life doesn't seem worth living anymore. I feel trapped, and I'm so tired of it. I'm tempted to kill myself, just to escape all this misery.

"I've lied to Mama and stolen things. I'm such a sinner already, and I'm afraid I'll wind up being just like Mama. I don't want to be like that. I want to be a sweet Christian like Juanita and have a good, happy life. But I can't do it myself. I need Your help. Change my life, Lord. Make it different. Help me, God. Please! Come into my heart and save me."

By surrendering her life to Christ, Sandi at last

found an anchor of hope for her storm-tossed life. Jesus brought peace to her troubled spirit, assuring her He understood. He had also experienced rejection and abuse, and He not only could, but would, answer her prayer and help her.

Although life would not be easy, somehow Sandi knew everything would eventually be all right. She knew Mama's problems were the results of her own choices and not because of anything Sandi had done. Sandi also knew it must break the heart of Jesus to see Mama ignore Him, after He had loved her enough to die for her. But Sandi was not doomed to follow Mama's lifestyle. She could trust God to bring her safely through.

Chapter 19

"Guess what, girls!" Mama's face glowed. "I found an apartment! We can finally move out of this camper and live in a house again."

"Where?" the girls asked together.

"Over in Arcadia," Mama smiled.

"Oh, Mama. That means changing schools again," Sandi's face fell.

"Well, yes, I suppose it does," Mama admitted. "But that's nothing new. You can go to school anywhere."

"But then I can't finish the year with the concert choir," Sandi lamented. "I worked so hard to get into the choir, and now I'll miss the big tour and everything."

"Now Sandi," Mama whined. "You know this camper isn't big enough for all of us. And soon there will be another one. I'm having José's baby, so we are going to get married. Surely you wouldn't want to pass up this chance for an apartment just so you can run around singing with your friends."

When they moved, Sandi had to admit living in an apartment instead of a camper was a big improvement for them, even though at first they sat on lawn chairs and slept on the floor. The apartment complex had a swimming pool, which helped compensate somewhat for the disappointment of dropping out of the concert choir and leaving her friends when they moved. The pool was a popular place with the tenants, and the girls found it a good place to meet the neighbors and try, once again, to form new friendships. Mrs. Carson, the owner of the apartment, hired Mama to clean apartments when tenants moved out, and get them ready for the new tenants.

The move meant the girls could no longer ride the church bus to Sunday school, but Sandi was determined to keep going somewhere. She found a Baptist church only eight blocks away, to which they could walk. The people were warm and friendly, and she soon found new friends. Still, she missed seeing her friend and role model, Juanita, every Sunday.

"Where do you think you are going?" José growled one Sunday morning, coming out of the bedroom only half dressed.

"To church, of course," Sandi said. "It's Sunday."

"Oh no, you're not," José grunted. "You didn't take the garbage out yesterday, so you can't go to church today."

"That's not true," Sandi shouted, even though

she knew it was no use arguing. José found sadistic satisfaction in depriving the girls of the pleasure of going to church, simply because he knew they enjoyed it.

The girls' absence, however, did not go unnoticed. Around noon, José answered the bell and found Sandi's Sunday school teacher and her husband at the door.

"We missed your girls at church this morning," Mr. and Mrs. Kaylor said pleasantly. "We just thought we'd stop in on our way home and find out why they weren't there. Is someone sick?"

"No," José grunted, too surprised to lie. "They had other plans this morning," he added lamely, not wanting to admit he had forbidden them to go.

"That's too bad," Mr. Kaylor said understandingly. "Well, I hope they can come next Sunday. We'll be looking for them."

José allowed the girls to attend Sunday school the next Sunday, but on the following one he again forbade them to go. This time the pastor came by asking for an explanation for their absence. And again, José hid the real reason behind a lame excuse.

Although the girls never told anyone about their home life, the church people soon understood the situation. From then on, someone dropped by every Sunday and walked with them to church. José did not have the nerve to say no when someone was there to accompany them, so they attended regularly.

"Come here, Sandi," Mrs. Carson called one afternoon when she saw Sandi crossing the courtyard on her way home from school.

Cautiously, wondering what was wrong, Sandi approached the owner of the apartment complex.

"Would you like to work for me?" Mrs. Carson asked. "I could use some help in the office."

Sandi's heart leaped. *A job! A real job!*

"I know you are still in school," Mrs. Carson went on. "This would be only on weekends. There would be various smaller duties, but mainly I need someone to work in the office renting apartments on weekends. Most people like to move on weekends, so you would help your mother clean apartments when people move out and then rent them to the new tenants. I would pay you $3.35 an hour. Do you want the job?"

"Oh, yes!" Sandi beamed. Then her face fell. "But what about church? Is it all right if I go to church Sunday mornings?"

"That will be fine," Mrs. Carson nodded. "You can work Sunday afternoons after church."

Mrs. Carson helped Sandi buy some appropriate clothes for work in the office. The business clothes belied her 15 years. Sandi loved the job and the feeling of importance it gave her. She was earning a good wage for her age, and this, combined with her mother's earnings, enabled them to buy some used furniture before Mama's baby was born.

Although José worked occasionally, he did not contribute to the family finances, but left it to Mama and Sandi to support the family.

Little Jimmy Perez made his appearance in March of 1977. With a dark complexion and black hair like José, he looked nothing like any of his sisters. Although the four all had the same mother, none looked alike because each had a different father.

Sandi took Jimmy into her heart the instant she took him into her arms. *I'm this innocent child's big sister,* she thought with a new joy as she realized he needed her. He gave her a reason to go on living. *I can endure the turmoil and fighting in this house, but I will not allow José to abuse this baby like he does the rest of us. Jimmy can't defend himself, but I'll protect him.*

"We're moving back to Oklahoma," Mama announced one day when Jimmy was about a year old. "I'm sick of California. I want to go home again."

"How will we get there?" Sandi wondered. "We don't have a car."

"We got a tax refund and I'm going to buy plane tickets with it," Mama said. "I called Aunt Carmen. She said we can live in their basement."

The family of six flew back to Oklahoma as Mama wished, leaving everything behind except the clothes they could carry. This was not a great loss since they had nothing of much value.

Sandi hoped living with Aunt Carmen would somehow improve their lives, but little changed. Although he never mistreated his son, José abused the girls just as he had before.

"You get your hands off these girls," Aunt Carmen snapped when she saw José hitting one of them.

"They're my kids, not yours," José retorted. "Mind your own business."

"They are NOT your daughters," Aunt Carmen shot back. "They are my nieces—my blood relation—and how you treat them IS my business."

The long, loud argument continued with no one getting anywhere. Soon Mama joined in the argument, adding to the noise and confusion.

Sandi hated the constant arguing and fighting. Someone was always yelling at someone else. It was either Mama and José, Mama and Aunt Carmen, José and Sandi, José and Aunt Carmen, or some other combination equally raucous. There was no peace anywhere in the house.

Although only a year had gone by, Sandi's assurance that God would help her have a different life seemed like ancient history. It looked as if nothing would ever change.

Chapter 20

After another bitter argument with Aunt Carmen, Mama decided to move out of Aunt Carmen's house. Not able to pay rent, she found an abandoned house in a rough section of town, and José did a few basic repairs to make it livable.

"Please, Mama," Sandi begged. "Let me stay with Aunt Carmen."

"No," Mama flatly refused. "You're going with us. What makes you think you're better than the rest of us?"

Sandi's heart sank when she saw the dilapidated two-bedroom house built into a steep hill. The floors, which slanted to the middle, were covered with old linoleum. There were holes in the walls and most of the window panes were broken out. The whole house was cold and drafty. José had boarded the windows with plywood, blocking out the light and making the rooms dark and dingy. The only cupboard in the kitchen hung on the wall above the white porcelain sink with only a curtain below it. The table was set in a cubby hole by the back door.

The move required another school transfer. This was the eleventh school Sandi had attended in her eleven school years. Like the neighborhood, the school was a rough place. The grounds and restroom floors were littered with trash. The walls were dirty and covered with graffiti. Although the building was not outdated, it was badly abused and in need of repairs. Drugs were routinely sold by students who carried knives and refused to study. The teachers spent more time trying to keep a semblance of order than they did teaching.

I've got to get out of this place, or I'll get killed, Sandi thought desperately. *I'll quit school and get a job somewhere.*

Finding a job was not very difficult. Sandi applied at Captain B's, a new fast-food restaurant, and was hired. The manager agreed to deduct installments from her paychecks for the cost of the red, white, and blue nautical type uniforms she was required to wear. She had no regrets when she left school for the last time to begin her full-time job.

The work was not difficult, and Sandi quickly learned to take and fill orders. She found a sense of fulfillment in being able to earn a paycheck, support herself, and help provide for the needs of the family. Her effort to do her best won her a promotion, and she began working in the dining room, cleaning tables and providing customer assistance.

When she discovered friendly helpfulness earned tips, she took up the challenge of seeing how many she could get.

Although Sandi's quitting school was an escape from a dangerous environment, it did nothing to improve matters at home. Everything there seemed to be going wrong. José continued his verbal and physical abuse of the girls, and was meaner than ever. Unknown to Sandı, he molested the younger girls while she was at work. Mama knew it, but did nothing about it. With Mama not on speaking terms with Aunt Carmen, the girls did not get to church anymore since their move.

It's completely hopeless, Sandi thought as she mechanically wiped a table. *For seventeen years I have lived on hope—hope that Mama will change and things will get better. I just can't go on like this anymore. It's time to stop hoping and start doing something. It's up to me to find a way to make a better life for Jimmy and the girls and get us out of this mess. In this state, girls my age can legally leave home. I can hardly bear to leave the children, but I have to so that I can help myself. I can't help them until I help myself.*

"Hi, Sandi," a girl's voice behind her said. "Since when do you work here?"

"Oh! Hi, Sheila," Sandi grinned as she turned and saw her second-cousin. "I've been here a couple of weeks."

"Really?" Sheila exclaimed. "Strange I never

saw you before. I come into this joint often. I don't live far from here."

"No, I didn't know," Sandi admitted.

"Yeah," Sheila breezed, "Got my own apartment awhile ago."

"Really?" It was Sandi's turn to be surprised. "I was thinking about doing that myself," she confided, "but I'm not sure I could make it alone."

"You can live with me," Sheila offered. "Would be real handy for you. You could walk to work."

"I'll think about it," Sandi promised.

"Just say the word," Sheila said, shaking salt on her fries and beginning to eat.

The more Sandi thought about her cousin's offer, the more it seemed like the way out. The only thing that held her back was a reluctance to leave her sisters and little brother. José would probably abuse the girls even more if she were not there to defend them.

But I have to help myself before I can help them, she reminded herself.

Now that an opportunity for escape had presented itself, Sandi found the constant yelling and fighting at home more unbearable than ever. After one particularly vehement battle with José, she suddenly knew she'd had enough. Taking immediate action, she went to the phone and called Sheila.

"This is it," Sandi announced when her cousin answered. "I'm leaving today."

"Okay. Get your stuff together. I'll come and pick you up," Sheila promised.

Sandi hurriedly packed her few belongings in a garbage bag and mentally prepared for the battle that was sure to come.

"What are you doing?" Mama snapped, when Sandi dragged the garbage bag to the front door.

"I'm leaving," Sandi announced stubbornly.

"What!" Mama exploded.

"I'm leaving," Sandi repeated. "I just can't take this kind of life anymore. You blame me for everything. I'm making you miserable, and I'm miserable too. There is always fighting, and I can't take any more of it, so I'm leaving."

"You can't leave. I need you," Mama said, switching to her helpless tactic as her eyes filled with tears.

"I'm sorry," Sandi said firmly, "but I am going."

"If you leave, you'll be leaving the children. How can you stand that?" Mama cried, hitting what she knew was Sandi's tender spot.

"That is your job," Sandi countered. "I can't do it anymore. You can." It was always difficult to refuse Mama when she cried.

"If you leave, you can never come back," Mama threatened, cursing Sandi. "You'll never see the children again. And don't go running to Aunt Carmen and live with her, either. When you walk out that door, you are OUT."

Mama threw her words like a dagger at Sandi's

heart. The rejection cut painfully, and Sandi burst into tears. But she was determined not to change her mind. Leaving seemed her only hope for a better life.

Mama continued to rant and threaten even as Sheila helped load Sandi's bag into the car trunk. With a last tearful glance at Mama, Sandi got into the car. Joining her, Sheila slammed her door, started the car, and tore out of the driveway.

In a way, Sandi was glad her sisters were in school, so they did not have to witness the scene. But at the same time, she ached to tell them good-by and see them one last time.

Sandi had been promoted to night supervisor, working the evening shift until midnight. Since she was afraid to walk to work, a coworker living in the same apartment complex often gave Sandi a ride.

"You drive," Kelly said one night, sliding over to the passenger side.

"I can't," Sandi objected. "I don't have a driver's license."

"Well, I'm not fit," Kelly groaned. "I got stoned, and I'm still too shaky. Go ahead and drive. It's not far."

Terrified to be driving without a license, Sandi complied. She could see Kelly was in no condition to drive and wondered how she expected to work. Driving once without incident made it easier to do it the next time Kelly was drugged or drunk. Soon

Sandi was driving frequently.

Kelly was a pleasant person, but she had a miserable life. She lived with a man and tried to pretend she had a real home, but it was an illusion. The man did whatever he wanted, and Kelly's only choices were to put up with him or hunt another place and try to make it on her own.

The poor girl is so unfulfilled, Sandi thought sadly. *It's so easy to fall into these traps and mess up your life. I'm not taking just any man that comes along. I want a man I can trust, one who will love only one woman. But are there any like that? I hope so, but I've never seen one .*

By now, Sandi was doubting the wisdom of having moved in with Sheila. The apartment complex was a rough place, known as a den for drug dealers. Sheila and her friends were a reckless crowd who drank and used drugs. Sandi had never indulged in those kinds of things and was dismayed at the wild parties Sheila hosted. When Sandi resisted the insistence of Sheila's friends that she join their revelry, they mockingly labeled her "the good girl."

At first, Sandi ignored their taunts, knowing they did not expect her to party and drink with them. But the constant mockery was difficult to ignore and made her feel like an oddball.

"I am so tired," Sandi moaned at the end of one long workday.

"One of these will fix you up," Sheila said, holding out a small white pill.

"What is it?" Sandi asked doubtfully.

"Just a little something to pick you up," Sheila said.

"I don't know," Sandi hesitated.

"Oh, come on," Sheila taunted. "Don't be such a goody-goody. It's no different than taking an aspirin for a headache."

"All right," Sandi decided, reneging her Christian principles. "I'll try it."

Sandi was not prepared for the intense effects of the speed pill. It did more than eliminate weariness; new sensations began possessing her. She felt powerful, yet detached from herself and not responsible for her actions.

"Watch this!" Sandi sang out. Picking up a full jar of mayonnaise, she threw it across the room with diabolic strength. The glass jar shattered into fragments, and mayonnaise splattered onto the wall and floor.

The sound of the breaking glass somehow penetrated Sandi's foggy mind. She sobered enough to stare, horrified at the mess she had created.

That's enough of that! Sandi decided, sick with disgust at herself. *I'll never do that again! Whatever possessed me to do it even once? I hated when Mama took drugs, and I don't want to be like that. This is no place for me. But what can I do? I'm trapped. I can't go back to school, and I have to work. I'm doing things I should not do, and I'm not*

*living right, but I don't know how to help myself.
I've got to get out of here before I wind up being
something I don't want to be.*

Sandi began searching for a place of her own.
Finally she located a small apartment she could
afford on her minimum wage paycheck, but the
landlord required a $100 security deposit which
she did not have. Not knowing where else to turn,
she decided to go see Grandpa. Cousin Robbie, who
hung out with Sheila's crowd, took her across town
to see him.

"I'll admit I was angry at first when you left
home," Grandpa told Sandi as he wrote out a
check. "But now I see it differently. I want to help
you make it on your own."

Oh! I can't do this, Sandi thought the next day
with a sudden change of heart. *I can't take money
from Grandpa. Why did I even ask him?* Tearing
the check in small pieces, she dropped it into the
trash can. *Now I'm back where I started,* she
thought ruefully. *I don't know what I'll do, but I
just can't take money from Grandpa. He'll think I
am using him the way Mama always did.*

Sandi continued to mull over the problem of
where to live until one day when she confided in
Robbie.

"That's easy," Robbie drawled. "Come live with
Mom and me."

"I can't," Sandi objected.

"Why not?" Robbie was baffled.

"Mama told me not to," Sandi said simply.

"So?" Robbie hooted with laughter. "You don't have to listen to her. You can do what you want. Besides, she just moved to New Mexico with José. She doesn't care what you do, or she would have taken you along with the rest of the family."

Sandi suddenly felt very foolish. There had never been any reason why she could not have lived with Aunt Carmen. But, accustomed to obeying Mama, she simply never thought of it as an option. The only reason Mama had told her not to go there was because she was jealous of Aunt Carmen. She knew Aunt Carmen loved Sandi and would take good care of her, reducing the chances of Sandi returning home.

"Yes, of course," Aunt Carmen answered sympathetically when Sandi posed the question. "You don't want to live like Sheila and her crowd. I wish Robbie would stay away from there too. Pack your things and come right over."

"Well, if you really want me, I'll come," Sandi decided, relief evident in her voice.

"Of course I want you," Aunt Carmen replied. "Get your stuff and leave a note for Sheila so she'll know where you've gone."

Sandi hurried to comply. At last, her prospects were looking brighter.

Chapter 21

Life in Aunt Carmen's house was more peaceful than anything Sandi had known in a long time. Aunt Carmen helped her get a new job in a department store and took her to work. With Robbie, they were usually a family of three, since Uncle Ralph was a long-distance truck driver and seldom home.

Aunt Carmen helped Sandi buy a used car, but Sandi refused to get a learner's permit until it was totally paid for. On Sundays they attended Aunt Carmen's Baptist church. The people were friendly and made Sandi feel at home. It was so good to be able to go to church again.

Although things were peaceful for the moment, Sandi was not fully content. She was terribly afraid of being a failure and repeating her mother's mistakes. Her life seemed to be at a dead end, and she did not see much hope for change.

I'll never be able to get anything more than a minimum wage job without a high school diploma, Sandi thought. *I'll never get far in life myself, so how did I think I would ever help my family? I'm doomed to marry Donnie, even though I don't really like him, because he is the only boy my age at church.*

"Oh, God!" Sandi cried out, "I'm not going to make it. I've done all I can do for myself, and it's not enough. I've gone as far as I can go alone. I want something better. I want to live a godly life. Please help me! Show me what to do."

The girls at church were all excited about the coming week of church camp and were making plans to go. Sandi had never been to camp and entertained no visions of going now. Listening to the girls' chatter emphasized the difference between their lives and hers. Although she did not feel excluded, she felt her lack of a proper home separated her from them in things like this which they accepted as a normal part of life.

"Sandi, would you like to go to camp?" the pastor's wife, Rosa, asked her privately.

"Yes, of course," Sandi admitted. "But I can't."

"Why not?" Rosa asked.

"I don't have the $50 it costs to go, and I couldn't get off from work for a week," Sandi replied.

"Someone from church will pay the $50," Rosa promised. "See if you can get off work."

"Well, I'll try," Sandi said hesitantly.

The more she thought about it, the more Sandi wanted to go to camp. From listening to the girls' talk, she knew as many as 600 young people would be there for the week. Daily Bible study classes were held in addition to recreation and crafts. The opportunity to spend a week in Bible study appealed to her even more than the other activities. She requested the week off from her job and waited to see what would happen. One week before camp was to begin, her request was granted.

"I can go!" Sandi reported exuberantly to Rosa. "I got the week off."

"Great!" Rosa rejoiced with her. "I'm sure you will enjoy it immensely."

"I can hardly wait," Sandi breathed.

No longer was Sandi a silent listener to the conversations about camp, for now she was going too.

"Lord," Sandi prayed as she packed with growing anticipation, "I am going to camp to learn more about You. Would You please give me some direction during that week about what I should do with my life? I promise You I'll not waste my time chasing boys or anything. I will spend the time in sincere Bible study and searching for Your will."

Camp Winton proved to be even better than Sandi had dreamed. A four-hour drive from her home, it was situated in a secluded wooded area by a large lake. The boys and girls were housed in separate groups of cabins on opposite sides of the camp with the dining hall, chapel, and recreation areas scattered through the center of the campgrounds. Sandi shared a cabin with a counselor and six other girls.

Bible classes were held every morning and evening with social and recreational activities sandwiched in between. While Sandi enthusiastically participated in all the activities, the Bible studies remained the main attraction for her.

On the way to chapel one morning, Sandi stopped short when she focused on the T-shirt of a tall young man approaching her. "Freeport Baptist Church," she blurted out without thinking. "Is that where you are from?"

"Yes," the young man smiled down at Sandi.

"My grandparents live about a block from that church," Sandi announced, and marched off toward the chapel.

Now that's interesting, Philip thought as he walked on toward the chapel. *I wonder who she is. She won't be hard to recognize again because of her eye. I wonder what happened. She certainly doesn't seem to let it bother her.*

Hungering for spiritual truth, Sandi found a front-row seat in every class. She listened and asked many questions, drinking in all the Bible teaching with an unquenchable thirst. After several days, she began to feel guilty for talking so much in the Bible classes.

I better stop hogging the class, she thought as she came to class one morning. *After all, the others here want to learn too. I'll sit in the back row this time and just listen. Someone else should have a turn to sit up front and ask questions.*

Harry, the Bible teacher, opened the class period with prayer. "Philip," he said to a tall young man from his home church, "would you please close the back door? That wind is blowing in too hard."

Philip got up and closed the door. When he turned to go back, someone had taken his seat. The only seat left was in the back row, next to Sandi.

Sandi looked up and smiled politely at him as he folded his lanky frame into the seat. He nodded slightly in return. *The girl with the blind eye!* he thought, recognizing her.

He's handsome! Sandi thought, not remembering she had met him on the path a few days earlier. *But he doesn't have a Bible. There must be something wrong with a person who doesn't carry a Bible to a Bible class.* She did not realize he had left his Bible at his former seat.

"We will begin this morning with a few verses from Philippians 3," Harry announced.

Sandi fumbled with the pages until she found the passage in her Bible. Since Philip did not have his, she shared hers with him. After Harry had read the passage, he began asking about the meaning of the verses. Philip took Sandi's Bible and quickly flipped through it to find the answer.

Sandi's unfavorable first impression of Philip changed quickly when she saw how well he knew the Bible. He seemed to know the answer to every

138

question. Not only that, he knew where to find passages in the Bible and turn to them quickly.

He knows so much about God, Sandi thought in awe. *I am so thirsty for God and know so little. Will I ever know God and my Bible like that? I have so much to learn.*

After the Bible class, a group from Sandi's church was scheduled to give a small program. A hum of conversation and anticipation filled the room as the group arranged themselves. Sandi craned her neck, but could not see.

"Can you see if there are any empty seats up front?" Sandi asked.

Philip stood up and scanned the front rows. Well over six feet tall, he towered a foot over Sandi and could easily see over the heads of the crowd.

"Follow me," he said, and strode up the aisle.

Sandi trailed the young giant to the front row. He leaned down and whispered something to a boy sitting there. The boy scooted over to make room, and Sandi sat down. She turned to smile her thanks, and found Philip sitting down beside her.

Oh no! Sandi groaned to herself. *He's got the wrong idea.*

"Thanks very much for finding a seat for me," she whispered to him, "but you don't have to sit with me."

"Oh, I don't mind," he whispered back.

He misunderstood my intentions when I asked him to find a seat for me. He thinks I'm flirting. I promised God I would not chase boys at camp. He will be disappointed with me. What shall I do? she wondered. Although she had wanted the front seat in order to see better, she was too preoccupied with her new predicament to get much out of what was given.

The program lasted until lunch time. At dismissal, Sandi immediately headed for the door. She sensed Philip was following her down the aisle. As she started toward the dining hall, he fell into step beside her.

"You don't have to walk with me," Sandi tried to brush him off. "You probably want to walk with your friends."

"Oh, no. That's fine. I'd rather walk with you," Philip said.

Not wanting to hurt his feelings, Sandi voiced no further objections. They joined the lunch line and got acquainted while they waited and as they ate. She learned he was from another part of the same town in which she lived, and his home was only one block from Grandpa Gilmores. They discovered they had at one time attended the same school, but since he was in first grade when she was in kindergarten, they had never met. When they finished eating, they deposited their paper plates in the garbage can and left the dining hall.

"It was nice meeting you," Sandi said. "I'll be going now. I'm scheduled to play volleyball."

"Fine. I'd like to watch your game," Philip said.

Not knowing how to send him away tactfully, Sandi said nothing. She was painfully aware of him watching her as she played. When it was over, she saw him coming toward her.

"I am playing next," Philip grinned down on her. "Since I watched your game, now you must watch mine."

"All right," Sandi consented, not knowing what else to do.

Philip's height, added to his agility, made him a skillful player. Sandi could not help being impressed with his ability on the court and was not surprised when his team won.

"Good game!" Sandi complimented him. "I'll see you later. I'm going swimming."

"A swim would be great after a game like that. Walk with me to my cabin and wait until I get ready. Then I'll go with you to yours and wait while you get ready," Philip said, not wanting to let her out of his sight a minute for fear she would purposely disappear.

"Okay," Sandi agreed with mixed emotions. The more she saw of him, the more she was attracted to him. She wanted to be with him, and yet she did not see how she could be without breaking her promise to God.

Carefully hiding her thoughts as they walked toward his cabin, Sandi very honestly answered all of Philip's questions about her, even adding details he did not ask about.

"I was never very smart in school," Sandi volunteered. "My mother was out running around with men and drinking all the time. I had to take care of my sisters, so I never had much time to study."

Philip was impressed. Many of the girls at camp, obviously there to find boyfriends, fluttered around the boys, trying to impress them. He considered such girls wimpy and prissy. Sandi was different. She had been absorbed in the Bible classes. She was open, honest, and down-to-earth, telling things the way they were, even if it did not put her in a good light. *This girl is unique!* He thought.

"Here comes my brother," Philip said in a low voice as a shorter version of Philip appeared on the path. "Richard, meet my new friend, Sandi," he said when they met. "Her grandparents live about a block from us."

"Really?" Richard said politely as he shook Sandi's hand.

"Sandi, this is my younger brother, Richard," Philip made the formal introduction. "We're going to go swimming," he informed his brother. "Where are you going?"

"Canoeing," Richard answered.

"Okay, see you around," Philip said as they parted ways.

Philip was as good at swimming as he was at volley-ball. But, uncomfortable with the situation, Sandi struck out across the lake, deliberately trying to keep a distance between them.

We don't have to stay together to swim, just because we are in the same lake, she thought.

Long after Philip climbed out onto the bank, Sandi stayed in the water. She hoped he would get tired of waiting and leave, but he sat, patiently waiting, until the lake was nearly empty of swimmers. Knowing it would be rude to stay in any longer, she finally waded ashore.

"Well, I have to get ready for evening church," Sandi said after they had exchanged some small talk and started to walk away.

"I'll walk you back to your cabin and wait while you get ready," Philip announced.

Sandi tried to be sociable as they walked back to her cabin, all the while feeling she had made a fool of herself. She took a very long time getting ready, praying about the situation, not caring that Philip was sitting out in the hot sun waiting.

"You look nice," Philip smiled in approval when she finally came out. "Walk with me to my cabin now and wait while I get ready."

Philip did not need nearly as much time to get ready as Sandi had taken. They were soon making their way together to the chapel for the evening service.

"Nice to see you two together today," Sandi's pastor, Neil Freeman, greeted them at the door. "I've met Philip before," he said to Sandi. "He's a very nice young man. I highly recommend him."

143

Sandi's face flamed. *Great!* she sputtered indignantly to herself. *Now everyone has the wrong idea. I'm not supposed to be getting involved. God is really going to be angry.*

Philip found seats in the chapel for Sandi and himself, and they enjoyed the evening song service. When it was over, Philip led Sandi away from the crush of the crowd leaving the building and heading for their cabins.

"It's been great spending the day with you, Sandi," Philip smiled. "I'd walk you to your cabin, but it's off limits after dark. Have a good night."

"Good night," Sandi said simply, and turned to walk away.

"I'll see you tomorrow," Philip called after her.

Sandi made a face in the dark, knowing he could not see, and did not reply.

Chapter 22

Absorbed in her own troubled thoughts, Sandi did not see the pastor's wife approaching until she spoke.

"Sandi! I was hoping to run into you before you go to your cabin," Rosa said warmly.

Sandi looked up. "Oh. Hi," she said listlessly.

"I was so happy to see you with Philip today," Rosa said softly.

"Well, I'm not sure I was happy to be with him," Sandi countered.

"Why not?" Rosa asked in astonishment. "He is a very nice young man. I think any girl would be thrilled to have him notice her."

"Oh, I like him," Sandi admitted. "But I didn't come to Camp Winton to find a boyfriend."

"But Sandi," Rosa chided, "what better place is there to meet a Christian young man than at camp?"

"You don't understand. Before I came to camp, I asked God to give me some direction about what I should do with my life. I promised Him I would spend the time studying the Bible and learning more about Him. I promised not to chase boys or anything like that, but to use the week to seek His will for my life. If I get involved with Philip, or anyone else, I will be breaking my promise to God, and God will be disappointed with me."

"Sandi," Rosa said gently, "maybe God is bringing you and Philip together. Think about that. Maybe Philip is God's answer to your prayer."

Sandi scuffed the toe of her sneaker in the dirt of the trail as she rolled this new idea over in her mind. She did not know what to think, and even less, what to say.

"Pray about it tonight," Rosa encouraged her. "Ask God to show you His will."

"I will," Sandi promised. Thoroughly confused and heavy-hearted, she walked slowly back to her cabin.

The cabin, as usual, buzzed until lights out with the talk and laughter of six girls comparing notes on the day as they prepared for bed. Preoccupied with her problems, Sandi heard very little of the conversation. Finally, everyone settled down and fell asleep.

Alone on her bunk in the quiet darkness, Sandi sat with her chin resting on her knees and hands clasped around her ankles. She tried to sort through all that had happened that day.

Philip is kind and gentle. And he's so smart! she thought. *He loves the Lord and knows so much about God. Someday God will probably call him to*

*be a preacher or something special. I could learn so
much from him. But I wouldn't be fit to be a
preacher's wife. It wouldn't be fair to him, either, to
have a wife that is so dumb. And it would be cheat-
ing God to break my promise not to get involved
with any boys at camp.*

Sandi wrestled with her problem for hours as
the night wore on. She could not deny she was
attracted to Philip. The depth of his Christian
character and commitment drew her more than
his looks and athletic ability. "Lord," her heart
cried out desperately, "I want to keep my promise,
but I need love too. I can't make it on my own. I
want to have a Christian husband and live a godly
life. Is Rosa right? Did You bring Philip into my
life? Is this thing of You? I don't know what to do.
Please show me Your will. Philip said he would see
me tomorrow. I'm afraid he will want to be with
me all day again. What shall I do?"

"You came here for an answer," the Lord
seemed to speak to Sandi's open, seeking heart. "I
am trying to give you one. Don't be afraid to take
it. And as far as your promise—I know your heart,
and that's what is important. It's all right."

By now, most of the night had passed. But at
last, a great peace filled Sandi's heart and calmed
her troubled mind. In the morning, she was ready
to face both the day and Philip without fear.

Excitedly, Sandi dressed for breakfast, half
expecting Philip to come by the cabin to walk with

147

her to the dining hall. When the last of the girls left the cabin and he had not come, she gave up and went alone.

He's probably there waiting for me, she thought.

But when she got to the dining hall, no Philip was in sight. Sandi watched and waited outside the building as the long line inched forward. When the last person in line was entering the building and Philip still had not come, Sandi gave up and tagged along at the end of the line.

I guess he got the message yesterday, she decided sorrowfully. *I made a very foolish mistake and chased him off.* She was too disappointed to realize how ironic it was that the very thing she had tried so hard to accomplish the day before was now the last thing she wanted to happen.

As Sandi stepped inside the door of the dining hall, her heart leaped. There was Philip, sitting with some little girls at a table near the door. He saw her and smiled a greeting that banished all her doubts.

"Get your breakfast and come sit with me," he invited.

"Okay," Sandi agreed, with a smile that said more than her voice.

"Where were you?" Philip asked as she sat down with her tray. "I waited and waited for you."

"Where were you?" Sandi challenged. "I waited until the end of the line, and you didn't come."

"We must have been on opposite sides of the

building," Philip laughed. "I forgot there are two lines. I finally decided you were staying away on purpose because you didn't want to see me, so I gave up and came in."

"I did the same thing," Sandi laughed merrily. "I thought you changed your mind and didn't want to see me after all."

Laughing about the situation helped put the young couple at ease and started the day comfortably. They stayed together all day again, but this time Sandi did not try to get away from Philip after every activity. As she learned to know him better, she was amazed at how easy it was to share her thoughts and feelings with him. Somehow, he seemed to understand in a way no one ever had before.

When it was time to get ready for the evening service, Sandi put on the best clothes she had brought to camp and carefully fixed her hair to make herself as attractive as possible for Philip.

When he came to the cabin to walk with her to the chapel, Philip carried a bunch of fresh flowers he had bought at the camp gift shop.

"I brought you some flowers," he said unnecessarily, holding them out to her.

"Philip!" Sandi choked. Her eyes swam with tears as her heart filled with emotion.

"Don't you like them?" he asked, puzzled.

"Oh! Yes. Yes!" she cried, coming to her senses and reaching out to accept the bouquet he offered.

"I love them," she whispered, nearly crushing them as she buried her face in the soft petals.

Philip looked down at her. The golden tints in her hair shone in the evening sunlight. As she lifted her head, a tremulous smile set her face aglow. Her sightless eye stared blankly at him, but the other one told him so clearly what she was thinking that there was no need for words.

"Wait a minute," Sandi said, unaware of what her face had revealed. "I should put these in water before we go."

I must be dreaming, Sandi thought to herself as the two of them walked to the chapel. *This can't be happening to me. I never knew there could be such happiness in this world.*

Since this was the last evening of camp, the service was a special one. At the close of his message, the speaker invited those who had never accepted Christ as their Saviour to come to Him. Those who responded to the invitation were led away to be helped by counselors.

As Sandi sat with her head bowed and her eyes closed during the invitation, she thought about Judy, who was not right with the Lord. Quietly, she left her seat and went up to where Judy was sitting.

"Judy, don't you want to do something?" Sandi whispered.

Startled, Judy looked up. "I can't," she answered, looking at the floor.

"I'll go with you," Sandi offered.

Judy hesitated. "No, thanks," she refused.

Sadly, Sandi went back to her seat. She was surprised to find Philip's seat empty and could not imagine where he might have gone.

When the service ended a few minutes later, Sandi walked around the auditorium looking for him. She stopped short when she saw him in the counseling room, praying.

Why is Philip in there? Sandi wondered in dismay. *What spiritual struggle is he having? Isn't he what I thought he was after all?*

Sandi waited quietly outside the counseling room until Philip finished. When he got up from his knees, he saw her and came out to meet her.

"Let's take the long way around and walk by the lake," Philip suggested as they left the chapel.

"All right," Sandi agreed quietly, seeing little groups of campers and young couples drifting slowly across the camp toward their cabins. "We have time to go that far before lights out."

"Sandi, I want to tell you that I just committed my life to the Lord in the prayer room tonight," Philip said when they were alone. "I gave myself totally to God to use however He chooses. I am willing to spend my life in the ministry or some type of full-time service or do whatever He wants me to do."

"Oh, Philip! That's wonderful!" Sandi breathed. "I'd like to do that too. Could I? Right now?"

"Why not?" Philip answered.

The young couple stopped under the spreading branches of a tall oak and bowed their heads.

"Lord," Sandi prayed. "I came to camp to learn about You and seek Your will for my life. You have answered in a marvelous way and I thank You. Now I am committing my life to you for Your service. I know I am not talented, but all I am and have belongs to You, and You may use me however You choose. I want to go wherever You send me and do whatever You ask. I just want to glorify You with my life, whatever that may mean and wherever it may take me. Amen."

"Amen," Philip echoed in a hushed voice.

The world seemed to stand still as Philip and Sandi walked slowly around the lake. The chirping of crickets sounded like music all around them. The full moon cast long shadows and spread a silver path across the water. Sandi's heart was so full from all that had happened during the week. Dedicating her life to God, as she had just done now, was the perfect climax.

"Everything is so beautiful, so perfect," Sandi breathed.

Philip stopped and looked down at Sandi. Oblivious to the beauty of nature, his eyes saw only her simple, trusting, loving heart, a beauty beyond nature.

"I wish we didn't have to go home tomorrow morning," Philip sighed. "But at least we don't live hundreds of miles apart. Give me your phone number and I'll give you mine. I'll call you when I get home and let you know when I can come to see you again."

The phone numbers and good-byes were exchanged that evening, because they would not see each other in the morning. Philip left Sandi at the path to the girls' cabins and walked away toward his own for the night.

As Sandi watched him go, she felt a mixture of emotions difficult to describe. As great as the longing for what she believed he could give her was the fear of reaching out to accept it. Long ago she had learned never to trust men. Surely she would wake up in her bed at home to find this week had all been a beautiful dream. This much happiness could not last.

Chapter 23

The four-hour ride home from Camp Winton passed in a flash while Sandi's thoughts were occupied with Philip. She could picture perfectly his long, lithe frame; his sun-bleached blond hair; his bronze tan; his eyes that appeared to change color depending on what color clothes he wore; his kind, gentle nature; and most of all his love for the Lord.

She sighed. *Was he real? Would she ever see him again? Or had she imagined the whole thing?* She looked down at the bouquet he had given her and could hardly wait to tell Aunt Carmen what had happened.

When the church bus pulled up at Aunt Carmen's house, Sandi saw her aunt in the garage. Without taking time to collect her luggage, Sandi hopped off the bus, ran into the garage, and hugged Aunt Carmen.

"Aunt Carmen, guess what!" Sandi exclaimed.

"You met someone special!" Aunt Carmen laughed.

"I did! I really did!" Sandi squealed.

154

"I can see it written all over your face," Aunt Carmen laughed again. "What's his name?"

"Philip," Sandi said almost reverently.

"Philip what?"

Sandi's eyes widened. "I don't know," she gasped. "I never asked him."

"So here you are, back from camp, star-struck in love, and you don't even know his last name," Aunt Carmen chided.

"I'll ask him when he calls," Sandi brushed the oversight aside and launched into a description of Philip. She could not sing his praises long or loud enough.

"I can't wait to meet him," Aunt Carmen said when she could get a word in edgewise.

"He really is too good to be true," Sandi bubbled. "But you'll see he is everything I said and more."

Sandi floated through the next day, barely aware of what she was doing as her emotions alternated between elation and despair. One moment she was sure Philip would call her, and the next she was just as sure she would never hear from him again. By nine o'clock that evening she was exhausted and in bed, fast asleep.

"Sandi," Aunt Carmen called softly, knocking on her door a half hour later. "Someone is here to see you."

Sandi groaned and threw on her housecoat. Barefooted, she padded out to the living room.

"Philip!" she shrieked, catching her breath in a

strangled cry. She turned and dashed back the hall to her bedroom to make herself presentable. Standing just inside the door, Philip grinned at her embarrassment. At Aunt Carmen's invitation, he sat down to wait for her to return.

"I thought you would call before you came," Sandi said when she returned properly dressed.

"I came over for a basketball game on short notice," Philip explained. "I didn't have time to call, so I thought I'd just drop in a little. Sorry if I made a mistake."

"Oh, that's quite all right," Sandi assured him, overjoyed that he had actually come so soon. "I assume you and Aunt Carmen have gotten acquainted?"

"Yes," Philip nodded. "We had a nice little chat while you got dressed."

"I told her all about you," Sandi confessed," and she could hardly wait to meet you. Did you tell your parents about us?"

"Yes," Philip nodded again.

"What did they say?" Sandi was anxious to know.

"Well," Philip answered slowly, "I just said to Mom, 'What would you say if I told you I got a girl-friend at camp?' And she said, 'I'd scream and pull all my hair out.' So I didn't say any more. I have one more year of high school to go yet, and my parents have their hearts set on me going to college to be a minister. They don't want me to think about girls for a long time yet. To them, that would mean the end of all their plans and dreams. I'll take you home to meet them in a couple weeks. Maybe by then they will get used to the idea of a girl in my life."

"Well, we aren't getting married yet," Sandi said practically without thinking of proper protocol. "Of course you must graduate from high school. We're young and have lots of time."

Philip called Sandi frequently during the week and came to see her on weekends, more often attending her church than his own. He got an after-school job at a hotel only three blocks from where she lived, so he could see her every day either before or after work. His parents realized there was no way they could stop the growing relationship, even though Philip and Sandi were too young to think of marriage.

"Well, here we are," Philip said, pulling into the driveway of a two-story house in a development full of identical houses. "The Hanson home where I grew up."

"Oh Philip! I was so eager to meet your parents. But now that we are here, I'm scared," Sandi's voice quavered.

"Don't worry. I know they will love you, and everything will be all right," Philip assured her as he opened the car door.

Philip was right. After hearing so much about Sandi, his parents were eager to meet her in person. That first meeting helped calm some of their fears and left them cautiously optimistic.

The more Sandi saw of Philip's home, the more she considered it a model of security and stability.

The house had been one of the first built in the development, and the Hansons had lived there all of Philip's life. They valued the nice neighborhood and its good school.

The family had a close relationship with Philip's grandparents who lived close by. The family followed a regular routine, which included eating meals together at a regular time. Philip's father had worked at the same place as long as Philip could remember. He took the boys camping and to the Boy Scouts. He taught them to help other people and do what was right. Although he did not go to church himself, he wanted his children to go and helped his wife get them ready on Sunday mornings.

Philip's mother was a sweet, easy-going person. Although she was careful not to show favoritism, she had great dreams for Philip. After seven childless years of marriage, she believed his birth was a miraculous answer to prayer. Like Samuel's mother, Hannah, she had prayed for a child and had dedicated him to God.

Richard, whom Sandi had met at Camp Winton, was born sixteen months after Philip. Beth, was born nine years later. The Hansons seemed to take their normal, middle-class home for granted. Sandi could only try to imagine what it would be like to have a whole family living together in the same house all their lives. The normalcy and security of their family life was what she had always longed for.

Sandi and Philip's months of courtship were the happiest time Sandi had ever known in her life. Sometimes she struggled to accept the love Philip offered her. On the one hand, she thought he was perfect and deserved someone better than she, and on the other, she could not quite believe Philip would not eventually disappoint her. In her experience, hoping for better times had always ended in bitter disappointment.

"Sandi," Philip said tenderly. "You have lived with neglect, abuse, and violence for eighteen years. It may take that long for all the fear and terror to dissolve. Give yourself time and try to trust me. I promise I will not let you down."

Slowly, Sandi learned to trust him and believe he really loved her for who she was, regardless of her background and inadequacies.

Chapter 24

"**S**andi, let's go see what they have in the bridal department," Aunt Carmen suggested as the two of them were Christmas shopping in a department store.

"Okay," Sandi agreed, though the suggestion surprised her.

She knew it was not possible for her to have a formal church wedding. If and when she got married, it would be only a simple ceremony without any frills. But dreams are free, and she enjoyed browsing.

"Why don't you try this one on?" Aunt Carmen suggested, holding out a gown.

"Try it on?" Sandi was shocked. "I don't have any use for such a gown. I could never afford a church wedding."

"Oh, but you must have a church wedding," Aunt Carmen declared. "It doesn't have to be an elaborate wedding, but we can manage to see that you have a nice wedding. Go on, let's try it on you."

In the dressing room, Sandi dreamily lifted the gown over her head and put her arms in the sleeves. She could picture herself moving slowly down the church aisle toward Philip.

"Oh, Sandi! You are lovely," Aunt Carmen declared. "It's a perfect fit."

"But Aunt Carmen," Sandi protested weakly, looking longingly at her reflection in the full-length mirror. "I'm not even engaged. I'd die of embarrassment if Philip found out I bought a wedding gown! And I don't have the money. I can't buy this gown."

"Philip doesn't have to know anything about it," Aunt Carmen contended. "And we can put it on lay-away. It's on sale today. If you wait, it will probably be gone or else you will have to pay a lot more for it."

"Well . . ." Sandi hesitated, her resistance melting like snow in June. "But don't breathe a word to Philip."

Aunt Carmen paid $20 to have the gown put on lay-away. Sandi's mind whirled with dreams as the two conspirators left the store. She felt foolish for having done something so rash, knowing it could be years before she got married. Philip might find someone else and drop out of her life. The thought gave her the chills. She would want to die if that happened.

"I am so tired, I don't feel like doing anything," Philip yawned that evening. "What do you say we just stay home tonight?"

"Fine with me," Sandi agreed. She knew Philip

161

carried a heavy work load as a senior in high school, and besides being involved in track, drama, and debate teams, he was holding a part-time job. She could never have done all those things and still be an honor roll student as Philip was. Needing five tries to pass her driver's license test served to confirm Sandi's feelings of inferiority.

"I was so embarrassed yesterday," Sandi commented. "The lines of grouchy shoppers are so long this time of year, so I started praying for each person as I waited on them. That helps keep me from getting grouchy myself. Anyway, I was just finishing my prayer when I handed this man his bag. Instead of saying 'Have a good day,' like I usually do, I said 'Thank you, Lord.'"

"What did he say?" Philip yawned sleepily.

"He said, `I've been called a lot of things already, but this is the first time I've been called Lord,'" Sandi laughed.

"Did you tell him why you said it?" Philip asked.

"No, I was too embarrassed," Sandi confessed.

"It could have been an opening to witness to the man," Philip murmured, only half awake.

"Yes," Sandi agreed. "But I didn't think fast enough."

"Hmmm," was Philip's only answer. He was falling asleep.

Sandi looked at the clock. *It isn't that late,* she thought as she curled up on the end of the sofa. *Let him sleep a little. I'll wake him up when it's time to go home.*

The ringing telephone jarred Sandi awake. As she answered it, she saw it was past midnight.

"Is Philip there yet?" Philip's father asked.

"Yes, just a minute," Sandi answered, handing the receiver to him.

In no uncertain terms, Philip was informed it was past his curfew and time to get home. Guiltily, Philip explained to his father and beat a hasty retreat. There was no time for lingering good-byes this time!

On Christmas Day, Philip gave his long, blonde hair an extra swipe with the comb as he finished getting ready to go see Sandi. He slipped a little square box in his pocket and picked up a long, white florist's box with a dozen red roses nestled inside. Tense with apprehension, he approached his parents in the kitchen.

"Mom and Dad," he said, clearing his throat nervously. "I just wanted you to know I plan to ask Sandi tonight to marry me."

"That's no surprise, Philip," Mom said gently. "I expected it."

"How did you know?" Philip asked, surprised.

"I was putting clothes in your drawer last week and saw the box with the ring under some of your clothes," Mom confessed. "At first I thought I had found my Christmas present. But then it struck me—this isn't for me, it's for Sandi."

"Is it all right with you?" Philip asked, looking

163

at his parents.

"I wasn't very happy when I found the ring," Mom ventured. "But I told Dad, and we've had some time to think about it."

"And what do you think?" Philip probed.

"You know we want you to go to college," Dad stated.

Philip nodded. "There are lots of married people in college. Getting married doesn't mean I wouldn't go."

"People who marry young often miss it in their marriages," Dad pointed out. "We feel you are both too young."

"But Sandi and I love each other so much," Philip declared. "I know we don't have much money, and it will be tough for us with me in college. But if we can just be together, that is all we ask."

"You are both of legal age, and if you are determined to get married you can do it without my signature," Dad said. "I won't forbid you to get married now, but I wish you would wait until you are older. Things might be much more difficult than you imagine. I still think you are rushing into this too fast, but we wish you the best."

"We want you to be happy," Mom smiled through her tears as she hugged him.

"We will be," Philip's voice boomed with an assurance born of inexperience. "I know we will."

With Mama and José still living in New Mexico,

Philip asked Uncle Ralph for permission to marry Sandi.

"Certainly," Uncle Ralph beamed, granting the request. "May you have a long and happy life together—and may all your troubles be little ones," he added with a chuckle.

Life seemed a bed of roses as Sandi and Philip set their wedding day for July, between his high school graduation and entrance into college. Thorns were found among the roses, but those were to be expected and could not destroy the young couple's happiness. Aunt Carmen was delighted to play the role of "mother-of-the-bride" and enjoyed helping with wedding preparations. Sandi chose yellow for her wedding color, not because it was her favorite, but because she thought it would please both Aunt Carmen and Mama.

Philip's graduation from high school passed and only three weeks remained until the wedding. Sandi saw no clouds on the horizon to dim her hopes. But at the back of her mind a tiny fear nagged that it was too good to be true. Something was bound to spoil it.

Chapter 25

"Sandi," Mama's voice pleaded, "please come to New Mexico and get us. I've had it with José, and I want to come home. We don't have any money. You're our only hope."

"All right," Sandi sighed. "I'll see what I can do. I'll call you back and let you know."

If Mama was finally ready to leave José, Sandi felt it was her duty to go and rescue the family as quickly as possible. When Sandi talked it over with Uncle Ralph and Aunt Carmen, they agreed to take her to New Mexico to bring Mama and her children home.

The trip to New Mexico was made without delay. The little adobe house in which Mama and her children lived was in a sad state of disrepair, and none of them were sorry to leave it. Once again Aunt Carmen took in her twin sister's family, letting them live in her basement. Mama filed for a divorce from José to end her fifth marriage.

Sandi's sisters, now in their early teens, were delighted to be back in Oklahoma in time to attend

Sandi's wedding. She was glad, too, that they were home, but the addition of four people to the household quickly disrupted the pleasant atmosphere. Quarrels and all-out fights once again became routine. Philip was aghast when he heard the yelling and fighting.

"That's how Mama always is," Sandi shrugged. "I can stand it for another two weeks until the wedding."

"That isn't necessary. Get a trash bag and put your clothes in it. We're leaving," Philip announced in a voice that carried above the din of the fight.

There was a sudden deathly quiet. Everyone looked at them, stunned.

"What did you say?" Aunt Carmen demanded.

"You can't take her away," Mama objected, abandoning her previous fight and ready to start a new one.

"Oh, yes, I can," Philip said emphatically. "She—WE are not going to live like this. We are leaving right now. Come on, Sandi, let's go pack your stuff."

"Where are we going to go?" Sandi asked as Philip backed her car out of the driveway.

"To my home," he answered. "I'll ask my parents if you can live with us until the wedding. If they don't agree, then we will go to a Justice of the Peace and get married right away. We have the marriage license and there is nothing to stop us. You just are not going to live like that. You've had to put up with that all your life, and you don't need to take another minute of it."

Philip's parents wanted Sandi and Philip to have the church wedding they had planned. So they agreed to allow Sandi to live with them the last two weeks until the wedding. They were very good to Sandi and helped with the final preparations. Mom Hanson and Sandi baked the cake together and had a friend come in to decorate it the day before the wedding.

Sandi fingered one of the napkins stamped with "Sandi and Philip—July 18, 1981." It seemed like a dream that she would actually be married to Philip in a church wedding the next day. In a way, it would be a relief when the whole thing was over. Sometimes she wished she had never listened to Aunt Carmen's idea of having a church wedding. Trying to please her assortment of parents and relatives had been enormously frustrating.

As the strains of the wedding march pealed out from the organ, Sandi put her hand on Uncle Ralph's arm to begin their trip down the aisle. She could see Mama sitting on the front bench with Aunt Carmen and her sisters and brother. Her father had not come because he was offended that she had chosen Uncle Ralph to give her away.

Sandi's heart was in her throat as she took the first step down the aisle toward the altar. She could see Philip, standing straight and tall, waiting for her. She was close enough now to see the expression on his face. She smiled tremulously. His soft eyes spoke quiet reassurance.

After Uncle Ralph gave the bride away, Pastor Neil proceeded with the ceremony. Solemnly, Philip and Sandi repeated their vows to each other and knelt for prayer.

"The bride and groom have requested a special time of prayer and blessing," the pastor announced. "During the singing of the next song, anyone who cares to may come up and pray with the bridal couple or give them special counsel or blessing."

One by one, friends and relatives came forward to share with the bridal pair as the youth pastor softly sang "The Wedding Song."

At last, the long-awaited words of Pastor Neil, "I pronounce you husband and wife," concluded the ceremonies. Beaming, they turned to face the audience.

At the front bench, Sandi pulled a yellow rose from her bouquet. Bending down, she hugged Mama and handed her the rose. She gave another to Aunt Carmen, while Philip presented one to his mother. Together again in the aisle, Sandi placed her hand on Philip's arm, and they fairly flew to the back of the church to receive congratulations from the guests.

The reception in the church's social room was modest, with little more than punch and cake served cafeteria style. Philip would have preferred something more elaborate for his darling bride, but Sandi was far from disappointed. It was beyond her wildest dreams just to be cutting a tall, white cake. She was too excited to feel like eating anyway.

Mama, aloof and dour, was not able to smile for the photographer. She was peeved because Sandi had also given Aunt Carmen a rose from her bouquet.

"Sandi," Pastor Neil whispered in her ear while Philip was occupied with one of his friends. "Philip gave me ten dollars for doing the wedding. There is an old tradition that the minister gives the wife the money the groom gives him. So here you are. That's your money now," he winked conspiratorially and walked away.

That's funny! Sandi thought. *But bless him! He probably didn't know we had only $20 between us without this. Now we can have a $30 honeymoon.*

"Oh Philip, I just had an idea," Sandi bubbled when Philip returned to her side. "Let's stop by the hospital and take Rosa a piece of wedding cake. I know she was disappointed she couldn't come to the wedding. Could we?"

"Of course," Philip agreed instantly. The pastor's wife had had to miss the wedding due to minor surgery.

Leaving the reception in a shower of rice and good wishes, Sandi and Philip drove to the hospital in their wedding clothes and personally delivered the piece of cake to Rosa. She was delighted to know they cared enough to take the time to see her on their special day.

"I could have eaten that cake myself," Philip laughed as they left the hospital. "That reception wasn't enough to feed a bird."

"Stop and get something to eat before we go to our motel," Sandi suggested.

Philip shook his head. "It'll take all our money to pay the motel."

"I have $10," Sandi smiled, not saying how she came to have it.

"A woman of miracles!" Philip proclaimed and leaned over and kissed her soundly.

Still in their wedding clothes, and too much in love to care what anyone thought, Philip and Sandi went through the drive-thru at a fast food shop nearby. Then, bearing a bag of hot food, they entered the motel for their one-night honeymoon.

The next day the newlyweds returned to Philip's home. When they opened their wedding gifts, they were happy to discover $500 in cash, an unexpected bonanza. Feeling rich and well equipped, they headed toward college on Monday morning.

Chapter 26

Getting settled into the routine of the Baptist University was an exciting adventure for the newlyweds. They stayed in the dorm for a week until they found a trailer available for rent close by. Moving in was simple, since they had only their personal possessions and wedding gifts to put in place.

Sandi looked around the tiny kitchenette and adjoining living room with joy. Having a home of her own was a dream come true. For the first time, even though it was just a rented trailer, she felt she truly belonged. She was through being dragged from place to place without any say.

The bothersome problem of needing money was solved when Sandi found a job in a nursing home. She would much rather have stayed at home, but that was not possible. Her housekeeping needed to be done in the evenings while Philip studied.

"Bah!" Philip shattered the quiet one evening, slamming his notebook shut. "I'm sick of this garbage."

"Philip!" Sandi turned from the sink to look at

her husband in shocked surprise. "What's the matter?"

Philip threw his pencil down on the notebook as though placing an exclamation mark on his comments. "When I came to the university to prepare for the ministry, I expected to study doctrine and theology, to learn more about God and the Bible so that I can preach clearly and help people come to know the Lord. It seems all they're teaching us is how to get placed in a big church and make lots of money. They are making it a business, not a ministry. I feel like quitting."

"You can't quit," Sandi objected. "Your mother would be so disappointed. She always dreamed of your being a minister."

"I know," Philip sighed, running his fingers through his bushy hair. "But there's more to it than that. You know it isn't working out the way we had hoped. Your paycheck just isn't enough to make ends meet. It's not fair that you have to work and struggle to earn the living while I sit and study. It's my responsibility to support you."

"I don't mind," Sandi reassured him.

"You haven't complained, I know," Philip admitted. "But we've been here almost a whole semester, and the longer it goes, the worse it's getting. And the more I'm hating college," he added. "I feel like I'm wasting my time and money here."

"What would you do if you did quit college?" Sandi asked.

"I don't know," Philip groaned. "It's humiliating to go crying to my parents, but I don't know what else to do. We've got to do something; we can't go on like this. We're so far in the hole we have to look up to see the bottom."

Although Philip's parents were disappointed when he told them he wanted to drop out of school, they offered to take the young couple under their roof until they could get on their feet financially. To be uprooted so soon from the cozy bridal nest of her dreams was also a disappointment to Sandi, but she bravely packed their things and went back home with Philip.

Philip soon got a job, but Sandi found time hanging heavily on her hands with neither a job nor housework to keep her occupied. She decided to attend some classes in preparation for taking a GED test, hoping to get a high school diploma in fulfillment of one of her life's goals. Although she did her best to understand the material being reviewed, she found herself hopelessly lost.

"I'm sorry, I'm just not going to make it," Sandi told the instructor at the end of one of the classes. "I missed so much in school. I never learned this stuff."

"How old are you?" the instructor asked.

"Nineteen," Sandi answered.

"If you possibly can, I would suggest you go back to school," the instructor said kindly. "Public high schools are required to provide education to anyone under twenty."

"Really?" Sandi had not known the possibility of returning to school even existed. "I'll talk to my husband about it," she promised.

Philip enthusiastically endorsed the idea of Sandi's return to school. But she felt strange the first morning she reentered school as a student. Being older than the others and married, set her apart from them.

With diligent effort and Philip's help and encouragement, she earned passing grades and graduated in the spring. Receiving her diploma, even though a year later than it should have been, gave Sandi a great sense of accomplishment.

"I knew you could do it," Philip hugged her, as pleased with her achievement as if it had been his own.

"Thanks to your tutoring," Sandi stretched up to kiss him.

"I have some good news," Philip grinned. "Are you ready for it?"

"I can take good news any time. Tell me quick," Sandi demanded.

"I found a little upstairs apartment we can rent for $185 a month, utilities paid. I think we can afford that much now," Philip said. "What do you think?"

"Wonderful!" Sandi breathed. "Your folks have been good to us, but I can't help feeling we're imposing. The sooner we can have our own place again, the better."

"The best part," Philip added, "is that this place is close to your church where we were married, so we can attend there again."

"Oh, Philip! This is getting better and better," Sandi said joyfully. "I can't wait!"

Just as Philip had said, the apartment was tiny. It had only one bedroom, a small kitchen, a living room, and a bathroom. But it was a cute little place for two people, and they felt very fortunate to have their own home again.

Going back to Blue Lake Baptist Church was like going home again after a long journey. Although they had attended Philip's church while they lived with his parents, Sandi did not really feel at home there. The pastor's sermons were too scholarly for her to understand. At Blue Lake she was among her own friends again. Her soul thrived on Pastor Neil's clear preaching.

The congregation welcomed Philip and Sandi with open arms. Before long, even though Philip was only nineteen, he was asked to be the church's youth pastor. Located in a rough part of town called "the dog patch," the church had a wild bunch of young people desperately in need of help.

"I will accept the challenge of being youth pastor," Philip told the church board, "but under one condition. I will not accept a salary. I believe accepting a salary hinders a man's ministry."

"In what way?" the board chairman asked in

disbelief.

"I believe a salaried minister faces the temptation to tell people what they want to hear in order to keep his job. He is not as free to preach the whole truth of the Gospel. He also faces the temptation to move on to a church where he will be paid more. If I serve in the ministry, I want it to be a voluntary love service and not for money."

"Well," the chairman of the church board hesitated, clearing his throat and looking at the faces of the group around him. "What do the rest of you think?"

The brief discussion that followed ended in agreement that Philip could choose to reject a salary for his services. He felt the church board was amused by his convictions and was giving him a fatherly pat on the back, thinking he would eventually grow up and accept the way things were done.

Philip was licensed to serve as youth pastor, and two years flew swiftly by. Working with rebellious young people was both difficult and rewarding. Philip harnessed the energy of the rough, long-haired young men by organizing a basketball team. He earned their respect and cooperation by being both firm and kind.

Over and over, people told Philip he should go back to school and finish seminary training so that he could be ordained. Pastor Neil especially encouraged him to complete his education. Philip was not fully convinced he wanted to return to school, but wanting to please the people and feeling perhaps this was God's way of directing him, he at last enrolled in a school where he could work in exchange for his tuition. This was the only way the young couple could afford it.

Once again, Sandi found herself saying good-by to her church friends and her little home as she and Philip pulled up stakes and headed for another try at college life. This time it was more difficult to leave, for she had become attached to the apartment where for two years they had lived and made so many happy memories. But she had promised long ago at Camp Winton to follow God wherever He led, and this was but another step on the path.

Chapter 27

Sandi pitched a pile of boxes out the trailer door for Philip to dispose of and collapsed on the sofa. Everything was in place in their new home, and she was pleased with the results. She knew she would have to get a job as soon as possible, but that could wait until tomorrow. All she wanted now was a steaming bath and a bed.

Over breakfast the next morning, Sandi scanned the ads of the morning paper. "There are a couple of possibilities here," she mused. "But it would probably be the easiest to be hired at the factory."

"This sounds dumb," Philip hesitated and cleared his throat, "but I don't think I really want to go to college after all."

Sandi looked up quickly. "But Philip!" she protested. "That's why we came."

"I know," he said apologetically. "I said it sounds dumb to change my mind right after we get here, but I feel that if God wants me in the ministry, He will make that call known somehow Himself. Going to seminary seems to me to be taking things into my own hands; doing things to make things happen. I want God to reveal His will for me in His own time and way, whether that is being in the ministry or not. I just don't have peace in my heart about going to seminary."

"Well then, don't go," Sandi said simply.

"You know I never really wanted to go back to school," Philip went on. "I came only because other people told me that's what I should do. Now, the closer it comes time to actually go to class, the more I know I don't want to do it. I don't know how or when the Lord will call me to serve Him, but I believe if He wants me to be ordained, He will make it known without me doing anything to make it happen."

"You don't have to go to school if you don't want to," Sandi told him. "If you think it's not right for you, then don't do it. And don't worry about what people think."

"You really don't mind then if I don't go back to school?" Philip questioned.

"Not at all," Sandi assured him. "It's your life, and you are the one who knows best what God wants you to do."

"Well then, give me that paper," Philip grinned in relief. "If I'm not going to go to school, I'd better find a job."

Philip took a job at a lumberyard, and Sandi was hired at the factory. They saved as much as they could out of their paychecks, dreaming of

owning a home of their own in the country someday.

"How would you like to live on a ranch?" Philip
asked abruptly as he walked in the door one
evening.

Sandi turned quickly to face him. "A ranch? Are
you kidding?"

"Certainly not," he assured her. "I got a tip
today about a nine-hundred-acre ranch that's
available for rent only ten miles from here for $150
a month. You know it's always been my dream to
live in the country and this seems like the chance
of a lifetime to make a dream come true. What do
you say, Sandi?"

"It does sound good," Sandi admitted. "If you're
sure that's what you want, I'm willing."

It's not that I'm attached to this place, Sandi
kept her thoughts to herself as she packed up to
move once more. *We lived in this trailer only four
months. But I've been shoved from one place to
another all my life. I want to put down roots and
find a home where we can stay. But if this place is
the fulfillment of Philip's dream, it might finally be
the place where we can stay and not move again.*

Philip loved life on the cattle ranch. Sandi found
it quite different from the city life she had always
known, but it was a great satisfaction to her to see
Philip so contented and happy in his work. She
soon learned to love it as much as he did.

With the landlord's permission, they bought

some calves to raise. Philip and Sandi both found satisfaction in being able to point to something that belonged to them, even if it was only animals. Sandi found herself growing attached to some of the little calves she helped feed. Sandi found herself growing attached to some of the little calves she helped feed. Caring for them also gave her an outlet for her mothering instincts. Although they would have liked to have children, they were not overly concerned that there were none. Philip's parents had been married seven years before they had had children.

"Are you into a bike ride this evening?" Philip asked as they finished feeding cattle one day.

"Oh, I believe I can find that much ambition left in my bones," Sandi laughed. "It stays light so long these summer evenings; we should be able to go as far as the river and back before dark."

"I'll take my Bible, and we can have our devotions on the riverbank," Philip suggested.

"Sounds great," Sandi approved.

Pedaling side-by-side, the young couple rode leisurely toward the river. The chirping of crickets provided background music for their conversation as they discussed everyday matters. Working closely together on the ranch had strengthened their marriage, as it gave them plenty of time to talk and share their thoughts and feelings. In addition to being husband and wife, they found they were also best friends. This was the most secure and loving relationship Sandi had ever known.

"Let's sit over there," Philip said, pointing to a grassy spot after they had parked their bikes at the riverbank.

"All right," Sandi agreed, capping the water bottle and wiping her mouth with the back of her hand.

"It's so peaceful here," Sandi sighed, settling herself beside Philip with her back against a tree. "I just love living in the country."

"Ditto," Philip agreed, taking his Bible from his backpack.

"What are we reading tonight?" Sandi asked expectantly as he flipped the pages.

"John 15," he announced.

Sharing the Bible, they read the entire chapter aloud, the deep tone of Philip's voice alternating with Sandi's lighter one verse by verse. When they finished, Philip stared silently into the distance, contemplating what they had read.

"You know, Sandi," he began, hesitating before he went on. "Verses 1-6 clearly teach the opposite of the unconditional eternal security we were always taught. These are the words of Jesus Himself, and He said it is possible for a person to depart from Him."

"Read those verses again," Sandi requested.

"'I am the true vine, and my Father is the husbandman,'" Philip read. "'Every branch in me that beareth not fruit he taketh away: and every branch that beareth fruit, he purgeth it, that it may bring forth more fruit. Now ye are clean through the word which I have spoken unto you. Abide in me, and I in you. As the branch cannot bear fruit of itself, except it abide in the vine; no more can ye, except ye abide in me. I am the vine, ye are the branches: He that abideth in me, and I in him, the same bringeth forth much fruit: for without me ye can do nothing. If a man abide not in me, he is cast forth as a branch, and is withered; and men gather them, and cast them into the fire, and they are burned."

"For a long time, I haven't felt comfortable with the idea that once a person is saved he is always saved no matter how he lives," Philip began trying to explain his understanding of the Scriptures. "I know that's what we were always taught, but I've been studying it, and I'm getting more and more convinced that is twisting Scripture.

"This illustration of the vine shows us our spiritual life comes from Christ," he went on.

"Verse 4 indicates the indwelling of Christ is dependent upon our choice. If we abide, or remain in Him, He abides in us. Just as a branch has to be connected to the vine to bear grapes, so we must be connected to Christ to bear fruit. Without Him we are powerless and useless. Verse 6 says any branch that does not abide in Christ is rejected and burned in the fire. Just as we have the freedom to choose to begin abiding in Christ, we also have the freedom to choose to stop abiding in Him."

"I don't understand these deep doctrinal things," Sandi admitted, "but common sense tells me if something is wasted, it will soon be gone. So wouldn't it be possible to be truly born again and then lose your salvation because you wasted it?"

"That's a simple way to put it," Philip smiled, "but you are exactly right. We become Christians through faith in Christ, but that relationship continues only as we continue to walk with Him. I believe we are secure in Christ. We don't need to be afraid He will cut us off the instant we make a mistake. But it is possible to sin away, or waste as you put it, the grace of God. We can't walk away from Him and still claim to be in Him."

"The Bible says it, plain and simple, and you can't argue with God's Word," Sandi said with finality.

"Well, let's pray and then head back home," Philip ended the discussion. "It will soon be getting dark."

Philip prayed first, and among other things, thanked God for His Word and asked Him to give them the grace to live by all its teaching.

Sandi's prayer echoed Philip's, but also included her daily prayer for Mama, who had married for the sixth time. Her sisters reported this husband was a convicted child molester who had served time in prison, and now abused them. Sandi's heart ached for her sisters and brother, and she prayed daily for their protection and deliverance from evil.

Chapter 28

"Smearing your face again?" Philip teased as Sandi applied her makeup one Sunday morning.

"Touching up, not smearing," Sandi contradicted.

"Your face is pretty enough just the way it is," Philip reminded her.

Sandi grimaced at him in the mirror. "This is a new church we are trying this morning. I must look nice."

"Doesn't make sense to me," Philip shook his head. "You spend more time trying to look pretty for strangers than you do for me. Seems to me people should look their best for those they love most. Only dead things need paint. You are alive in Christ. He makes you beautiful from the inside out, so that's all you need."

"I don't use much makeup," Sandi tried to justify herself. "But I can't go to church without any. Everybody uses it. Oh, Philip! I do hope this church is the one where we will feel at home," she sighed, changing the subject.

"Maybe it will be," he said without much enthusiasm.

"What's wrong with us?" Sandi sighed again. "Why can't we find a church we can commit ourselves to?"

"I don't know," Philip sounded discouraged. "I know all our friends back home think we are losing out spiritually because we haven't joined a church here."

"We're not losing out," Sandi protested. "We still read our Bibles and pray as much as we ever did. And Tim and Suzette started coming here for Bible study with us every week."

"We know where we stand," Philip agreed, "but I can see why those looking on think we're drifting. We've been on this ranch almost two years, and we're still not settled on a church. But I don't want to join a church just to have my name on a church roll. I want to join a church that practices the things the Bible teaches. Christianity must be part of a person's everyday life, not just something you do on Sunday mornings. All the churches we have attended seem so empty and ritualistic. People are out there grabbing all the money and things they can. They seem to have forgotten, or at least don't take seriously, what Jesus said about seeking His kingdom first and trusting Him to supply all our needs."

"We'll keep looking," Sandi encouraged. "Sooner or later we'll find a good, Bible-believing church.

God has never failed yet to provide what we need, and He surely won't fail to meet our spiritual needs now."

"Yes, of course," Philip agreed. "I just hope it doesn't take much longer."

The next morning the landlord called and announced the ranch had been sold. Philip was stunned; Sandi was heartbroken.

"I don't want to leave this place," she bawled inconsolably.

"I don't either," Philip comforted her, "but we have to."

"We've never lived anywhere longer than two years," Sandi sobbed. "I moved around all my life. I'm sick of it. Can we buy a house, so we'll never have to move again?"

"I don't know," Philip sounded doubtful. "We don't have much money—but we do have the calves. We'll have to sell them if we're moving. I'll see what they bring, and then we'll see what we can do."

Sandi was almost obsessed with the desire to own a house. In answer to her prayers, the calves brought a good price, and Philip and Sandi began house hunting. They knew they could not afford an elaborate house, nor did they want one. The place they finally found was an unpainted, hillbilly house. The sale of the calves had given them half of the required down payment. Philip's father agreed to give them the other half.

189

Sandi was ecstatic when the bank approved their loan and the papers were signed giving them ownership of the rickety, old house. The pain of leaving their ranch home was softened by the knowledge that this time they were truly settling into a house of their own and would not be forced to move again.

Leaving the ranch meant Philip was again unemployed. He was pleased to find work as an apprentice blacksmith in a nineteenth-century living history demonstration in a town nearby. The job didn't pay much, but it was a craft in which he had always been interested. Sandi supplemented their income by cleaning rooms at a motel and working at one of the concession stands at the living history demonstration. Together, they were able to meet their expenses.

"You look so nice when you put your hair up and wear long dresses," Philip remarked as he and Sandi drove home from work one evening. "I wish you would always dress like this."

"This isn't the nineteenth century," Sandi laughed. "Women have come a long way since then."

"And I'm not so sure it's all been for their own good," Philip said dryly. "A woman in pants just can't be much of a lady, no matter how she sits. I want my wife to be a lady, not just a woman."

"Does the Bible say a woman can't wear pants?" Sandi challenged him.

"Not in so many words," Philip admitted. "But 1 Timothy 2:9 says women should wear 'modest apparel, with shamefacedness and sobriety.' That means women should dress modestly and decently. Pants on a woman are not decent, because they're not modest. I'm sure the idea of women wearing pants didn't come from God, and I don't think they are appropriate for a Christian woman. It seems to me Christians should be identifiable by their appearance as well as their actions. And one way for a Christian woman to identify herself with Christ is to wear dresses. I wish you would wear dresses more than just for work."

"Well," Sandi agreed hesitantly, "if it will make you happy, I'll try." She had worn slacks and jeans as long as she could remember and had never thought about whether or not they were appropriate for a Christian. But because she knew the Bible taught a wife should submit to her husband, she agreed to Philip's wish.

Sandi loved the tumble-down house into which they had moved. Her natural talent for adding just the right touches without spending a great deal of money made it attractive and homey inside, despite the drab exterior. Philip good-naturedly allowed Sandi to decorate as she pleased. But when he came home one day and found holes in one of the walls, he could no longer remain silent.

"Sandi, what happened to this wall?" he demanded.

"What do you mean?" Sandi was puzzled.

"There are holes all over it," he said, pointing to several places.

"Oh, that," Sandi shrugged. "I was going to hang some stuff there, but after I had it up, it didn't look right, so I took it down again."

"What kind of nails did you use? Railroad spikes?" Philip asked.

"No," Sandi replied indignantly. "What does it matter what kind of nails I used? I pulled them all out again."

"But when you hammer a nail into the wall, it makes a hole," Philip explained patiently. "And when you pull the nail out, it leaves a hole where the nail had been. The bigger the nail, the bigger the hole."

"Oh!" Sandi said in a small voice.

"Be sure where you want to hang things before you hammer any nails in the walls. And use smaller nails, so they don't make such big holes," Philip advised.

"I'm so stupid," Sandi berated herself.

"No you're not," Philip smiled gently. "We're all ignorant; just on different subjects. You just know more about hammering than you do about carpentry.

"And now I have some exciting news," he changed the subject. "You know blacksmithing has gotten me interested in buggies. Well, there is another place near the blacksmith shop that is expanding. They want to add a buggy shop and asked whether I'd have it. I'd really like to do it. What do you think?"

"Oh! Philip! I think that would be great!" Sandi exclaimed.

"The only problem is I'd have to lay out a couple thousand dollars to get started," Philip said. "You know we don't have it. I hate to keep asking Dad for more money, but I want so badly to get into this, that I'm really tempted to ask him anyway."

"He can't do more than say no," Sandi said practically.

"We'll pray about it. If Dad says no, I'll know it's not for me," Philip said, reluctant to think of the dream slipping away.

Philip's father did not turn down his request, and Hanson and Son Carriage Company was soon operating. Philip thrived on buggy restoration and giving demonstrations to tourists. He enjoyed working with buggies as much as he liked meeting the public and working with people. The tourists appreciated his interesting dialogues and demonstrations of his craft. Completely happy with their lot in life, Philip and Sandi were both sure they had found their niche at last.

Chapter 29

"**I** met some intriguing people today," Philip said, forking a piece of chicken onto his plate.

"Umm?" Sandi's own mouth was too full to reply.

"You know that buggy shop I was going to go to in Mitchell today to get some supplies?" Philip asked without expecting an answer. "Well," he went on, "the man who operates it doesn't make buggies as antiques. He makes them for the people in his church. They drive them."

"Drive them?" Sandi echoed.

"Yes. Drive them," Philip repeated. "They don't have cars. They use a horse and buggy for transportation. And that's not all. They don't have electricity either."

"What kind of church is that?" Sandi asked in disbelief.

"It's something called Amish," Philip replied. "It seems they are a large group. The man seemed surprised that I didn't know about them."

"Never heard of them," Sandi shook her head.

"Neither did I," Philip conceded. "But I really would like to know more about them. They look so old-fashioned. The man I met wore suspenders and a straw hat. I saw his wife at the wash line. She wore a long dress and a white cap on her head. And they aren't doing it as a tourist attraction. It's the way they live. That's what fascinated me."

"Sounds strange," Sandi commented, and then changed the subject. "I talked to Mama today."

"Oh? What's new?" Philip asked.

"I finally cleared my conscience of a lie I told Mama years ago," Sandi confessed. "When I ran away from Dottie and my father, I made up a dreadful story about him so Mama wouldn't make me go back. It worked, too, but it's really been bothering me. I knew as a Christian, I must make it right."

"You did the right thing," Philip encouraged her.

"I'm certainly glad to be rid of the load," Sandi sighed with relief. "Sylvia is getting married," she said, switching subjects abruptly. "I want to go to her wedding."

"Of course we'll go," Philip promised.

Although Mama did not bother much with Sandi since she had married, Philip knew Sandi liked to keep in contact with her family and join them on special occasions.

Philip's continuing need for supplies and parts for his buggy shop periodically brought him into contact with the Amish people. Their happiness and contentment, in spite of their Spartan lifestyle, impressed him. Too embarrassed to ask questions about their beliefs, he simply observed.

One day, leafing through a mail order catalog from a hardware store in Ohio, Philip saw some books about Mennonites and Amish. Deciding this was the perfect way to learn about these mysterious people, he added two books to his order.

The books, *Twenty Most Asked Questions About the Mennonites and Amish,* and *By Birth or by Choice,* arrived about a week later. In the first book he learned that the Mennonite and Amish churches had begun in Europe in the 1500s and had come to America before the American Revolution. There are many variations of Mennonites and Amish, and not all of them live without cars and electricity. While the book provided some answers, it presented more questions to Philip's inquiring mind than it answered.

Picking up *By Birth or By Choice,* Philip began reading again. In this book, he learned the Mennonite church is composed of over 700,000 members scattered across 52 countries of the world. While the majority of Mennonites are people born into Mennonite homes, the church welcomes people of all backgrounds to join its faith and practice. The main purpose of the book was to invite anyone searching for Christian fellowship in a Biblical setting to consider becoming a Mennonite. More than a dozen people of various backgrounds shared their stories of how and why they had chosen to become a part of this church.

The back of the book contained an Appendix summarizing Mennonite beliefs. Philip read to the end with growing excitement.

"Sandi! Look at this!" he cried, leaping from his chair. "This is exactly what we believe!"

"What?" Sandi turned from the TV.

"These beliefs of the Mennonites," he said, shoving the book under her nose.

Startled, Sandi took the book and read the page Philip showed her. She did not understand all the doctrinal terms, but she understood enough to know he was right. The nature and existence of God, the fall of man, salvation through grace by faith in Jesus Christ the Son of God, the work of the Holy Spirit, living in conformity to Christ rather than the world, and more. It was all there, the same as they had come to believe through reading their Bibles.

"Sounds good," Sandi acknowledged. "But there's no Mennonite church around here, is there?"

"Not that I know of," Philip admitted. "I did hear there might be some around Greenfield or Billstown."

"Can we find them?" Sandi asked eagerly.

"I don't know," Philip said thoughtfully. "But there must be some way to find out."

Although they were both interested in learning

more about the Mennonites, Philip was more patient by nature than Sandi. He would have waited longer for something to develop naturally. But Sandi had never been satisfied to wait for things to happen; she had always forged ahead trying to make things happen.

"Look, Philip," Sandi said as she stacked the breakfast dishes one Tuesday morning when they both had a day off. "We keep talking about finding these Mennonites, but we don't do anything about it. They aren't likely to come knocking on our door. We've got to go find them."

"That's true," Philip conceded, "but how do you propose to go about doing that?"

"You said you heard there might be some around Billstown," she reminded him. "Let's go there and ask around. If there are Mennonites there, somebody will know how to find them."

"It's worth a try, I guess," Philip consented. "But before we do anything, let's pray and ask God to direct us. If He wants us to find these people, He will open the door."

After prayer, Sandi and Philip set out on their journey, trusting the Lord to reveal His will. The forty-five-minute drive to Billstown turned out to be the only successful part of the trip. Their inquiries about a Mennonite church in the town all brought similar answers. "Nope, can't say as I have." "Mennonite? Never heard of any hereabouts." "Not that I ever heard tell." And so on it went.

"It looks like this was a wild goose chase," Sandi admitted dejectedly after receiving another negative answer.

"We can't give up yet," Philip objected. "Let's pray again and ask God to show us what to do."

Oblivious to passersby, they bowed their heads and prayed for guidance.

"I know," Sandi said when they finished praying. "Let's find a pay phone and look in the phone book. If there is a Mennonite church around here anywhere, it might be in the phone book."

Philip drove slowly up and down several streets, but they could not see a phone booth anywhere.

"There's a Wal-Mart," Sandi pointed. "Let's go in there. They'll have a phone book at the information desk."

"Do you have a phone book we could borrow for a minute?" Philip politely asked the lady at the information desk.

"Certainly," the lady replied, pulling one from a shelf and shoving it across the counter.

"Thank you," Philip said courteously.

Philip and Sandi sat on the bench next to the information desk poring over the phone book in search of a Mennonite church. None was listed.

"Well, we prayed and we still can't find a Mennonite church, so I guess the answer is no," Philip said dejectedly. "Let's give the book back and go home. I guess that's that."

They returned the phone book and thanked the

lady again.

As they turned to leave, they were astonished to see a Mennonite lady walk in the door of the store. They stared at her as she walked past without noticing them.

"Go after her," Philip urged Sandi in an undertone. "Ask her where their church is."

"Ma'am, Ma'am," Sandi called, hastening after the lady. Catching up with her, Sandi touched her lightly on the shoulder.

The lady stopped and turned. "Yes?" she asked, wondering what this pony-tailed girl in the denim jumper, cowboy boots, and jangling earrings might want of her.

"Are you a Mennonite?" Sandi asked bluntly.

"Yes," the lady answered.

"My husband and I have been reading about the Mennonites," Sandi waved a hand at Philip who joined her. "We are interested in knowing more about them. Could we come to your church?"

"You would be welcome, I'm sure," the lady said. "But our services are in German. I don't think you would enjoy that very much—unless you understand German," she added.

"No. No, we don't," Sandi said, disappointment edging her words. *Everything has come to a dead end,* she thought. *I guess we may as well give up the whole idea. It's not for us.* "Well, thanks anyway," she said, starting to turn away.

"Wait a minute!" the lady said as an

afterthought. "There is a place called Rest Haven at Collings. They have services in English. It's actually a nursing home, but they also have church services. You could try them."

"We will," Philip and Sandi promised in unison, as smiles lighted their faces. "Thanks a lot!"

Fired with new excitement at this hopeful lead, Philip and Sandi nearly jogged out to their pickup and whizzed directly down to Collings. A man at a service station knew where Rest Haven was and directed them to it.

Pulling into the parking lot at Rest Haven, they saw the Mennonite secretary inside the office.

"It's a lady," Philip said softly. "You do the talking."

"No," Sandi protested, "you do."

"You talked to the lady in the store," Philip pointed out.

"I feel stupid now. I don't know what to say," Sandi explained.

"Well, they see us. We can't just sit here. We have to go in," Philip declared, opening his door and getting out.

Sandi followed him into the office. The secretary had left the room. A man seated at a desk looked up when the young couple appeared at the open door.

"May I help you?" he asked doubtfully.

"I don't know," Philip said, feeling foolish.

"Well, come in," he invited, "and we'll see what

we can do." Coming from behind the desk and shaking hands with both of them, he introduced himself as Homer Mast and asked their names.

"Have a seat," he said, waving a hand toward two chairs in front of his desk.

Philip and Sandi took the seats indicated, and Homer sat down behind his desk again.

"Now, how can I help you?" Homer asked kindly.

Hesitantly at first, Philip began telling the story of what they had read about the Mennonites and how their desire to learn more had brought them to Rest Haven. Sandi interjected her comments as he told the story, feeling it was important for Homer to understand that they were already Christians and not ignorant pagans.

"So," Philip concluded, "we were wondering if we could come to your services on Sunday."

"You certainly may," Homer said graciously. "Sunday school starts at 9:30 and preaching at 10:30. You're welcome to attend both."

"Thank you. We'll be here," Philip promised.

Chapter 30

"**O**h Philip, I'm sick as a dog," Sandi moaned, flopping across the bed weakly after vomiting in the bathroom. "I'm sure I have a fever. I can't go to church this morning. What should we do?"

"I don't know," Philip said softly. She was obviously unfit to go anywhere.

"We promised those people we'd come to their church this morning. What will they think if we don't show up?" Sandi lamented.

"Maybe if you rest a little you'll feel better," Philip encouraged.

But Sandi's condition did not improve.

"I think this is just Satan trying to keep us away from the church," Philip declared. "We can't let him get away with it. We have to go."

Huh! Sandi thought, *That's easy for you to say. You're not the one that's sick! But the more she thought about it, the more she felt Philip was right.*

Dragging herself out of bed, she got dressed for church. The nearer they got to Collings, the better she felt. By the time they got out of their pickup at

Rest Haven, her queasy stomach had settled down peacefully.

The words of the hymn the congregation was singing accompanied their entrance into the chapel:

"Great is Thy faithfulness! Great is Thy faithfulness!"
Morning by morning new mercies I see;
All I have needed Thy hand hath provided—
"Great is Thy faithfulness," Lord, unto me![1]

Sandi was entranced by the fervent a cappella singing. She had never heard anything like it before in her whole life. The four-part harmony was beautiful! *It sounds like angels singing,* she thought.

Inside, a family stood looking at the bulletin board, waiting for the song to end before entering the sanctuary. The man and his wife looked inquiringly at the long-haired, bearded young man and his wife who had just entered.

"Good morning," Philip smiled, politely shaking hands with the father. "My name is Philip Hanson, and this is my wife, Sandi. We met Homer Mast a few days ago, and he invited us to attend the service this morning."

"Glad to have you," the man said warmly. You are welcome to worship with us. I am Eli Glick, and this is my wife, Lois, and our children."

Because the singing had ended, Philip and Sandi only nodded acknowledgment and turned to

[1]*Great Is Thy Faithfulness* by Thomas O. Chisholm. ©1923. Renewal 1951 by Hope Publishing Co., Carol Stream, IL 60188. All rights reserved. Used by permission.

enter the sanctuary. Sitting together on the back bench, they observed the assembled group. None of the men wore a tie and all had their hair cut in the same neatly trimmed short style. The women, all wearing dresses and white caps, looked alike to the visiting couple. Homer was the only one who was not a total stranger to them.

Although the patterns and customs were strange and different to them, Philip and Sandi thoroughly enjoyed the service. Eli, whom they had met before the service, preached the sermon. He was a bishop from Mt. Pleasant and had driven two hours to attend the service. Philip was impressed with the message and nodded in agreement several times to things that were said.

When the service ended, people immediately began visiting with those next to them. Sandi looked up at Philip uncertainly, wondering what they should do next. They did not know any of the people around them.

"Glad to see you folks made it," a friendly voice said behind them.

Philip and Sandi turned to see Homer standing there with a lady beside him. He shook hands with both of them and introduced them to his wife, Esther.

"We'd like you folks to come home with us for dinner today," Homer invited. "Will you come?"

Philip and Sandi exchanged an astonished look, neither knowing what to say. In all the time they had attended their own church back home, they had never been invited to anyone's home for dinner afterwards. They could not understand why strangers would invite them for a meal.

"Did you have other plans?" Homer asked, seeing their hesitation.

"No," Philip answered. That question, at least, had an easy answer.

"Good! Then you'll come," Homer said as if it were settled.

"We'd love to have you," Esther interjected.

"Well—yes," Philip said jerkily, accepting the amazing invitation, "we'll come."

When Philip and Sandi followed Homer, Esther, and their children to their home, they found they were not the only ones who had been invited. Eli and Lois were there also with their children.

Esther soon had a simple but wholesome meal on the table, and everyone was seated, with the children scattered among the adults. Visiting as they ate, Sandi was amazed to see how smoothly the parents worked together to care for their children.

After the meal, the men took chairs out under the shade tree on the lawn where they continued talking. The women cleared the table, washed and dried the dishes, and visited in the house.

From the moment she had stepped into the house, Sandi had been looking over the rooms to see how these people lived. She was impressed with the Scripture verse mottoes on the walls, a new idea to her. Seeing Esther's microwave was a relief. If they had even a faint notion of attending this church, it was comforting to know she would not have to give up her microwave.

Sandi soon began to feel comfortable with these women. Even though they were dressed differently than any women she had ever known, she could tell they were normal with the same feelings as other people. They were so warm and sweet, and not weird at all. Esther even let Sandi hold her six-month-old baby girl.

In the presence of such friendliness, Sandi soon felt comfortable enough to talk, and she asked all kinds of questions about the beliefs and practices of these people. Out on the lawn, Philip was doing the same. His questions, however, were more of a doctrinal nature while Sandi's were on practical, everyday living.

The ride home was short with all Philip and Sandi had to tell each other. They agreed it had been a wonderful day. They were both favorably impressed with all they had seen and heard. Recognizing Philip as a sincere seeker, Homer loaned him a copy of the book, *Doctrines of the Bible*. All the next week, Philip read the book carefully, looking for error. There was no question about whether or not they wanted to attend the Mennonite church again.

The next Sunday when Philip and Sandi

entered the church, they felt a little less strange than they had before. This time they knew more of the people and the pattern of the service.

The adult Sunday school class did not use quarterlies, but studied directly from the Bible. The lesson for this Sunday was from First Corinthians, Chapter 11. Philip and Sandi listened with growing amazement as the doctrine of the headship veiling was taught. Although the rest of the class had heard this teaching many times before, it was the first time Philip and Sandi had ever heard it explained. They understood now that the white caps the women wore on their heads were not worn because of tradition; these people were observing plain Bible teaching.

"I can't believe I went to church and read my Bible all my life and never saw this before," Philip exclaimed as they discussed the Sunday school lesson on the way home late that afternoon. After another dinner invitation from a different family in the church, this was their first opportunity to share their thoughts.

"I don't know as much about the Bible as you do, but I never heard this taught before either," Sandi agreed. "The longer I listened, the more I was convicted about it. I felt guilty when we knelt to pray, and I didn't have anything on my head. I never felt that way before; but then, I never knew that was in the Bible. What do you think we should do about it, Philip?"

"I don't know," Philip admitted.

"I want to do everything God says," Sandi said. "But this is such a new idea, and I need time to think about it."

The invitations to dinner with church families continued each Sunday. Philip and Sandi did not know there was a designated host family for each Sunday, so they did not know what to think of these weekly invitations. But because of this hospitality, they learned to know people much more quickly than they would have otherwise.

Fellowship in this small congregation was the close, family-style variety. Everyone knew everyone else, and all of them were a vital part of making the church function. The Hansons never felt they were not accepted by anyone.

The better Sandi became acquainted with the women, the more she admired these new-found friends. In them she saw everything she desired for herself. Their sweet, gentle ways reminded her of Juanita, her childhood role model. She longed to learn the homemaking skills that seemed to come so naturally to them.

Sandi began asking God to show her what to do about covering her head. The more she prayed, the deeper the conviction became that she could no longer go bareheaded. She began letting her hair grow and wearing a scarf at home, but she did not wear it when she went to church because it was not what the other women wore. Wearing a visible symbol of submission to God and her husband made it impossible for her to wear jeans without being convicted of inconsistency. Knowing Philip's preference, she found the switch to wearing only dresses much easier than she had expected.

Philip and Sandi enjoyed attending the Mennonite church. Although no one pressured them, the many new ideas they faced in so short a time created an intense burden within them. The doctrine of nonresistance was especially difficult for them to understand. Always having been taught a solid God-and-country viewpoint, they struggled to understand the Biblical doctrine of total separation of church and state. They came to see that this was one of the main doctrines that distinguished Anabaptists from mainstream Protestants. But as they heard it explained, and as Philip studied on his own, the truth became clear. This was what Jesus and the Apostles taught and practiced.

In her heart, Sandi felt they had found the church they had been looking for, and that they would eventually join the fellowship there. But as much as she wanted to, she was afraid to take such a big step. Everything was so different.

Oh forget it! Sandi thought one day when she was feeling terribly mixed up. *What do I think I am? I'm tired of feeling like two different people. I just want to be ME.*

Going to the bedroom, she jerked her dress over

her head and threw it in a heap on the floor. Yanking open a drawer, she found a pair of comfortable old jeans and a baggy sweatshirt and put them on. Then she fixed her naturally curly hair into soft ringlets around her face and put on makeup.

There now! That looks like me, she thought, studying her reflection in the mirror. *Forget all those other ideas.*

Seeing it was time to pick up Philip at work, Sandi slipped on her cowboy boots and drove over to the buggy shop. The disappointment on Philip's face was plain the moment he saw her, but he didn't say a word of rebuke. The relief Sandi had felt at "being herself" again was now replaced with a terribly guilty feeling as her true motives hit her—*I'm embarrassed to look different from everyone else. I'm afraid my dresses and scarf will identify me as a Christian.*

I am betraying my Lord! Sandi thought with chagrin. *How could I do this? I'm so ashamed of myself.*

Chapter 31

L ike parched plants whose roots had found a
life-giving stream, Philip and Sandi soaked
up all the Bible teaching available at Rest
Haven, attending every service. With faithful
attendance, they formed many warm friendships.

"Would you like to attend the Family Fellowship
Meetings?" Homer asked Philip in the fall.

"I'm not sure," Philip replied. "What are they?"

"Churches from the states in this area get
together for a weekend of meetings every
November," Homer explained. "This year it is our
state's turn to host the meetings. It will be held at
the church campgrounds near Mt. Pleasant. I'm
sure you would enjoy them, and we'd love to have
you."

After some discussion, Philip and Sandi decided
to go, praying earnestly that the Lord would give
them some direction at these meetings.

Not wanting to miss anything, Philip and Sandi
set out early for the one-hundred-fifty-mile trip,
pulling a little camper trailer behind their pickup.
They arrived so early Friday afternoon, that only a

few people were at the campgrounds. Not knowing any of them, Philip and Sandi felt awkward and conspicuous. They could tell everyone was wondering who they were and why they were there. But no one welcomed them.

Eli and Lois Glick lived nearby. It was a great relief when they and some other Rest Haven friends arrived. Before long Philip and Sandi were beginning to feel a part of the group assembling for a weekend of spiritual enrichment.

The families who lived in the area opened their homes to provide lodging for families coming from a distance. When the Friday evening meeting was over, everyone except Philip and Sandi left the campgrounds to spend the night in homes. Although they had enjoyed the evening meeting, they felt estranged, left alone in their little camper. But, they reminded themselves, their primary purpose in coming had been to worship God and seek His will rather than making friends.

After the morning and afternoon sessions on Saturday, time was provided for recreation and fellowship. By now, Philip and Sandi were feeling more at home and making new friends. As Sandi passed the kitchen door, she met Lois Glick coming out.

"Hi, Sandi," Lois smiled. "We've run out of catsup. I'm going home for some more. Would you like to ride along with me?"

"Certainly," Sandi agreed without hesitation.

The two women chatted pleasantly as they rode the short distance to Lois's house. Reaching out warmly for acceptance had become an ingrained part of Sandi's personality, and Lois was a comfortable person to be with.

As Lois entered her storage room and picked up several quart jars of homemade catsup, Sandi stared at the rows of home-canned fruits and vegetables lining the shelves.

"Did you can all this?" Sandi asked in amazement.

"Yes," Lois answered offhandedly. "Our garden did well."

To Sandi the thought of raising and canning all this food seemed incomprehensible, but Lois gave it no special thought.

"Where did you stay last night?" Lois asked as the two women drove back to the campgrounds.

"In our camper," Sandi replied.

"Oh!" Lois exclaimed. "So that's who I saw going into the campgrounds with a camper yesterday. Wasn't it chilly sleeping in a camper last night?"

"Not too bad," Sandi shrugged.

"Well, that isn't right for you to be sleeping in a camper," Lois protested. "You should stay in a home too. I'm sure someone has room for you."

"Oh, we don't mind," Sandi insisted. "We don't want to impose on anyone."

"Maybe not," Lois allowed. "But I don't like it. It's not right for you to be here all by yourselves at night."

Lois took charge of the situation and made the need known to some of the women. After the evening service, Fred and Wanda Kauffman invited Philip and Sandi to their home for the night. Actually, they insisted, and Philip and Sandi accepted the invitation. Although neither Philip or Sandi mentioned it, both were glad to leave the campgrounds and stay in a home like everyone else.

When Philip and Sandi arrived at the Kauffman home, they found Amos and Mary Miller were also guests, as well as the Kauffman's daughter and son-in-law, James and Susan Stoltzfus.

"You didn't tell me you already had guests," Sandi accused Wanda, surveying the small crowd of adults and children in the living room. "Your house is full without us."

"There's always room for two more," Wanda chuckled. "You folks can have our room and we will sleep on the sofa."

"We can't take your bed," Sandi objected.

"You not only can, you will," Wanda laughed again. "We've slept on the sofa before, and it didn't hurt us."

Even though it was already past bedtime, the small group sat around visiting. The fellowship of the meetings drew them together as much as the Bible teaching, and they could not seem to get finished talking.

"My covering was so old I was ashamed to wear it to the meetings," Wanda said during the conversation. "I finally got some new ones made."

"I wear a covering," Sandi announced abruptly.

The women looked at her in shocked silence.

"Oh, not around you," Sandi hastened on, seeing their astonished looks. "I don't have a white one like you wear, but I wear a scarf at home because I know the Bible teaches women should cover their heads."

"Would you like to have a white covering?" Wanda asked.

"I'd love to," Sandi breathed. "How can I get one?"

"I have an extra one you can have," Wanda offered. "Come with me."

The women went into the bedroom where Wanda produced a new white covering, pins, and a comb. Sandi sat on the edge of the bed while Wanda combed her hair, showing her how to pin it up to fit under a covering. Meanwhile, the other women continued to visit so naturally, it seemed as though things like this happened every day.

"You have nice hair," Wanda commented, fastening a hairpin into the knot she had made in back of Sandi's head.

"I've been letting it grow," Sandi said. "At home, I wear it pinned up and covered with a scarf. But I thought it would be rude for me to wear a scarf to church, because it's not what you wear."

"Oh, that wouldn't have mattered," Wanda reassured her.

"There now. How does that feel?" she asked, placing the covering on Sandi's head.

"It feels good," Sandi said truthfully. "But my skirt and blouse don't look right with it," she added, looking at her reflection in the mirror.

"Some of my dresses might fit you," Wanda suggested. "You can try one on if you like."

Sandi agreed eagerly, and Wanda took several cape dresses from the closet. Although not her exact size, several fit well enough.

"Tell Philip to come in here," Sandi giggled self-consciously. She was excited, but too shy to go out and be seen by all the men.

"What do you think?" Sandi asked radiantly when Philip's big frame filled the doorway.

A slow grin spread across Philip's face. "Looks great to me," he said approvingly.

After everyone had settled down for the night, and Philip and Sandi were alone in the bedroom, they discussed the serious implications of attending the meetings the next day with Sandi dressed in plain clothing. To them, it would be making a public statement and a commitment, nothing to be done lightly. Unless they intended to continue, they would not begin. And if they began, there were other changes they knew they needed to make.

There was very little sleep that night for Philip

and Sandi as they talked and prayed for direction and strength to do what was right. By morning, they had agreed to take the step in faith. They still were not absolutely sure they were going to join the Mennonite church, but they knew there were some things they were going to do regardless, because it was Biblical.

In obedience to First Corinthians 11, they decided Philip would get a haircut as soon as they got home, and Sandi would wear a covering. They both agreed to adopt the plain clothing of their Mennonite friends because it was a practical way to apply the Bible's teaching in First Timothy 2, First Peter 3, and other Scriptures. This would include getting rid of Sandi's makeup and jewelry as well as their immodest clothing. They also decided to dispose of their television set. For a long time they had felt the majority of things shown on TV did not encourage Christian living, but never before had they considered actually getting rid of it.

With mixed emotions Philip and Sandi approached the campgrounds the next morning. While there was peace with their decision, there was also apprehension. How would they be received? They need not have worried.

"You look nice wearing a covering," Lois whispered, giving Sandi a hug when they met outside the chapel.

"Thank you," Sandi smiled bashfully, her heart

swelling with gratitude for the kind words and gentle understanding.

Lois's response voiced the reaction of the entire group. The change in dress indicated without words that Philip and Sandi were more than curious onlookers. Somehow, it dissolved the reserve of those who had not known them before the meetings. Everyone accepted them now as part of the group, and they could feel a new warmth in the atmosphere.

Leaving the meetings felt like a leap in the dark for Philip and Sandi. They were afraid their families and friends would reject them. But they knew they could not stay in the safe cocoon of the fellowship meetings forever.

As they finished packing up to leave, Wanda came to say good-bye. "We love you," she said, hugging Sandi.

Those three little words warmed and strengthened Philip and Sandi's hearts for the unknown that lay ahead.

Chapter 32

As soon as they got home from the Fellowship Meetings, Philip got a haircut. This was more difficult for Sandi to accept than wearing a covering and cape dress. To her, Philip looked like a shorn sheep, and she preferred the way he had looked before. In fact, she thought they both looked ugly, and she avoided looking at herself in the mirror as much as possible.

Armed with garbage bags, Philip and Sandi attacked the job of getting rid of the things they knew they could no longer wear or use as Christians. All jewelry, makeup, and the immodest clothing, was sorted out and stuffed into the bags for disposal.

"We have to take our wedding rings off too," Philip said when they had finished.

"Oh! I can't!" Sandi stared at him.

"The Bible says our adorning should not be 'with gold or pearls or costly array,'" he reminded her. "Wedding rings are jewelry, just as much as the earrings and other things we put in the garbage bags."

"I know," she admitted. "But my wedding ring is part of my marriage vow. To take it off seems like being divorced."

"Our promises to love and be faithful to each other as long as we live are what makes us married, not the rings," Philip pointed out. "We have grown up believing rings are a necessary part of marriage. It's hard for me to take mine off too, because of its sentimental value. But the love I have for you in my heart and my promise to be faithful to you remains unchanged, whether or not there's a ring on my finger."

"I knew we would come to this some day," Sandi said, her chin quivering. "I'm willing to take my ring off if you are, but please don't ask me to throw it away."

"Well," Philip decided, "we'll never wear them again, but let's just put them away in a little box for now. Perhaps later the Lord will show us what to do with them."

The TV presented the greatest problem. Junking it seemed wasteful, so they decided to store it in a closet until they could find a good way to get rid of it.

"We must go visit my parents," Philip told Sandi. "I don't want them to hear about our changes from someone else. I want them to see us, and I want to explain to them myself what we are doing and why."

"I hope it's not too hard on them," Sandi said

wistfully. "I don't think Mama will care much, but we will need to explain to her, too."

Dad and Mom Hanson were, naturally, quite surprised at the changed appearance of their son and daughter-in-law, but they graciously kept their thoughts to themselves and did not create a scene. Using the Scriptures, Philip showed his parents the passages on which their new-found beliefs and practices were based. Dad had always been very patriotic and found it especially hard to understand the doctrine of nonresistance.

"Well," Dad said at last, "I can't say I understand all you're saying, but you are adults, and you must decide how you want to live your life."

"You were already committed Christians," Mom said. "I thought you were all right the way you were. But if this is what you want, it's your decision."

Philip and Sandi were relieved Dad and Mom had taken the news so well, and that their fears of rejection and ridicule had been unfounded. Of course, they had not expected Dad and Mom to understand and accept everything the first time they heard it explained, for neither had they. Knowing that Dad and Mom's love was big enough to give them the freedom to follow their convictions was sufficient.

The visit with Mama was as Sandi expected. Mama found Philip and Sandi's interest in the Mennonite Church and their changed appearance a curious development, but it made no difference to her what Sandi did.

"You do your thing and I'll do mine," Mama waved it off lightly. "Sheri is getting married," she changed the subject.

As Mama went on telling the latest family news, Sandi again felt the old, familiar pain of rejection. In a way, Mama's lack of interest hurt more than if she had violently objected, for it told Sandi Mama really did not care about her. Any hopes she had had of helping Mama spiritually evaporated with her disinterested response.

Back home, Sandi found time hung heavily on her hands. Keeping house for two wasn't enough to fill her days while Philip was at work. She longed to know what was happening on the soap operas she used to watch on TV. With nothing important for her to do, the temptation became overpowering. Dragging the forbidden fruit out of the closet, she plugged it in, and once again was enjoying her favorite programs. Time flew by, and before she knew it, Philip was home from work.

"Oh! I didn't know you were home." Sandi jumped up guiltily when he walked in the door. "Please, don't be mad at me," she pleaded. "I was so bored with nothing to do. I just couldn't help myself."

"I know," Philip said understandingly. "I miss television too. Let's watch it just tonight. Then we'll put it away again."

223

Having gotten the TV out of the closet once, Sandi found it easier to yield the next day, and she got it out again. They struggled for weeks, trying to wean themselves from TV addiction.

"You've been watching it again," Philip accused Sandi one evening, laying his hand on top of the TV.

"How do you know?" Sandi demanded.

"It's still warm," Philip said simply.

"I'm sorry," Sandi said contritely. "The days get so long without it. I think I'll just watch the news, and before I know it, I'm watching everything. I don't want to, but I can't seem to help myself. What can we do?"

"We'll have to disable it," Philip decided. "I'll cut the plug off. That'll fix it."

The plugless TV remained dark and silent for about a week, but then there was something special Philip wanted to see. So he rewired it, saying they would watch only that program. But with the plug back on, the temptation returned, and they were soon back where they started.

"This thing has got to go," Sandi declared after another day of falling to temptation. "There is so much immorality and foul language I feel guilty watching it. But my curiosity to see what happens next gets the best of me, and I turn it on again. We'll struggle with it as long as it's in the house."

"You're right," Philip agreed. "But I hate to just throw it in the junk. That would be like throwing

$300 away."

After discussing the options, they decided to give the television to an elderly neighbor. He was as delighted to have it as they were to be rid of it. Later on they would look back and realize it would have been better to just put it out as the worthless piece of junk it was. But at the time, having it out of the house and knowing the battle was over at last was a relief.

Sandi turned to sewing as a way to fill up the time television had consumed. With the help of church friends she learned to make her own dresses. Learning to sew was frustrating, but she resolutely refused to give up. Her first finished dress was far from perfect, but she kept trying and slowly improved.

Philip brought home books, and they learned to pass the time with reading in the evenings. Reading good books fostered spiritual growth and stretched their minds. There was so much to learn and discuss that before long they no longer missed the TV.

Feeling more certain all the time that this was the church they wanted to become a part of, Philip and Sandi applied for membership at Rest Haven. They began studying the Eighteen Articles of Faith of the Mennonite Church in a class with John and Ann King, Homer and Esther Mast, and James and Susan Stoltzfus. These three couples took turns hosting the small study group of eight.

Sandi enjoyed the warm, loving atmosphere in these classes, and received satisfying answers to the questions she asked. More than anyone else, these three couples patiently discipled the young seekers of truth, and became their closest friends.

"I'm learning so much," Sandi confided as she and Philip drove home after a class. "I've been a Christian for years, but I am learning so much about what the Bible teaches in such a short time, that it seems I didn't know anything before."

"It does seem as if we are different people than we were before," Philip admitted. "It actually embarrasses me now when I think of some of the things we did in ignorance—like going swimming together the first day we met. How could we? But back then we had never heard of courtship standards to guard against immorality. And I know now why my parents weren't too enthused about our getting married when we did. We were too young and shouldn't have rushed into it so quickly."

"I know," Sandi agreed. "We really were young and ignorant. By all the statistics, our marriage was very high risk, and the fact that it didn't fail was due more to the grace of God than anything we did."

"And the kind of wedding we had," Sandi added after a pause. "At the time it seemed perfectly proper, but now I don't want anybody to see our wedding pictures."

"It wasn't willful disobedience," Philip said. "We just didn't know better. I am so thankful God has brought us to a better understanding of His Word."

"So am I," Sandi agreed. "And I'm sure I still have a lot to learn," she added, blissfully unaware of how soon she would be reminded of that.

"Sandi, I'd like to talk to you a minute," Susan said the following week, drawing Sandi away from the rest of the group.

Sandi looked up uncertainly when they were alone.

"I hope you won't be offended, but I thought somebody should tell you," Susan began hesitantly. "You probably don't realize what some of the words mean that you use, and that you shouldn't use them."

"What words?" Sandi was puzzled.

Gently, Susan repeated some of the bywords Sandi used frequently and explained why they were not appropriate in a Christian's speech.

"Read Psalm 19:14 and then look in the dictionary for the meanings of the words you're using," Susan suggested. "After that, decide whether you still want to use them."

Sandi was shocked. She had heard cursing and swearing all her life and did not consider it swearing to use bywords. Neither did she realize what it sounded like to these people. She was embarrassed to learn they cringed every time they heard her use them.

227

What next?! Sandi wondered, half provoked. *Is there no end to the things I must learn?*

But when she learned the meaning of the words she was saying, she knew she could not continue using them. Only by conscious, diligent effort and the Lord's faithfulness in reminding her when she slipped, was she able to eliminate the offensive words from her vocabulary. Eventually, she thanked Susan for speaking to her about it.

One Sunday morning that fall, Philip and Sandi's application for membership was announced at Rest Haven. Both of them gave personal testimonies of faith in Christ and were recognized as proving members with full membership to follow in six months.

On a glorious spring morning, Philip and Sandi arrived at Rest Haven to be received as full members. As they waited on the front bench, they thought about the events and changes that had brought them to this point. *God is so good,* thought Sandi.

When the moment arrived, the bishop asked them to stand together to be received into the church fellowship.

"Do you acknowledge and confess that you agree and are of one mind with us in the doctrines and faith of the Mennonite Church, and that you acknowledge and accept them as in accordance with the teachings of the Gospel; and do you promise by the grace of God and the aid of the

Holy Spirit to submit yourself to them and also to the rules of order and forms of worship and to remain faithful and obedient in the same until death?"

"I do," Philip intoned solemnly.

"I do," Sandi echoed sincerely.

"In the name of Jesus Christ and His church," the bishop said, "I welcome you to the communion and fellowship of this church and congregation, and to the church in general. As long as you are faithful and abide in the doctrine of His Word, you are His disciples indeed and shall be acknowledged as members of the body of Christ and a brother and sister in the church."

The bishop shook Philip's hand and greeted him with a holy kiss. "The Lord bless you and keep you," he said fervently, while his wife came forward and greeted Sandi.

Sandi's eyes swam with tears. She had begun to find security and acceptance in Philip's love, but the desire for the love and acceptance of an extended family had remained. That need was at last fulfilled in the family of God.

Chapter 33

Philip walked into the empty kitchen and set his lunchbox on the counter. "Sandi," he called, "where are you?"

All was silent. He walked to their bedroom door. Sandi lay sobbing, face down on the bed. "What's the matter, Sandi?" Philip asked tenderly, sitting down on the edge of the bed.

"It's my birthday," Sandi sobbed.

"Is that something to cry about?" Philip rubbed her back sympathetically. He could not follow her reasoning.

"Oh, Philip! Don't you see?" Sandi cried. "I'm thirty years old. I want children so badly, and my clock is running out. Why doesn't God give us a baby?"

"I don't know, Sandi," Philip answered gently.

"At first I didn't worry about not having children because your parents were married seven years before you were born. But we've been married almost 11 years now. I keep hoping and praying, but nothing happens," Sandi said between sniffles.

"God knows what He is doing," Philip assured her. "We don't need to understand; we just need to trust Him."

"I feel so empty and alone around the women in our church," Sandi sobbed again. "It seems they only talk about two things—their children and who is related to whom. I have nothing to say. We aren't related to anybody in this church, and we have no children. If I hear another sermon about mothers and the blessing of having children in the home, I think I will scream. I'm sure God knows I'm not fit to be a mother. That's why He doesn't give us a baby."

"And I'm sure that's not true," Philip contradicted her. "I thought we had worked through all this before and decided our childlessness is an act of God. We decided we will just wait on God, knowing He has a purpose and trusting Him to do what is best for us."

"I know," Sandi said, blowing her nose. "I want to trust God, but I'm not as patient as you. I'm tired of waiting, and I just know there's no hope. We've got to do something, or we'll be childless all our lives."

"You know we don't have the money for any expensive doctors," Philip reminded her. "The Great Physician is still the best One there is. Jesus promised to give us anything we ask, according to His will. If it's not His will for us to have a baby, He can heal the pain of childlessness Can't you trust Him?"

"I'll try," Sandi promised. "But my faith is so weak."

Slowly, Sandi felt an unexplainable new hope rising in her heart. As the summer wore on, she became increasingly convinced God was going to do something important in their lives. It was as though a door had opened a crack, but not enough to see through to what lay on the other side.

The pulpit at Rest Haven had been filled with visiting ministers for a long time. The time had come, the church decided, to ordain a minister from among them.

Special meetings were called, and the members were asked to name their nomination for minister.

"Two men have been nominated," the bishop announced at the close of the voting. "They are Jonathan Yoder and Philip Hanson. We will use the lot to determine God's choice for ordination."

The week between the voting and the ordination was a stressful time for Philip and Sandi. They felt unworthy to take leadership in the church, but they were willing to accept it if that was the Lord's will for their lives. Their days were spent in prayer while they went about their normal duties and waited.

The phone was ringing as Sandi came in from her garden with a bucket of tomatoes. Setting it down, she reached for the phone. She had no idea how long it had been ringing.

"Hello, Hansons," she said into the receiver.

"Sandi! I almost thought you weren't home," the voice on the other end of the line said. "This is Esther Yoder from Madison. I just had to call you! Today when I was at the market with sweet corn, I got to talking to a lady from Hargrove. She said she knows of a woman with twin boys she wants to give up for adoption. She said the boys desperately need a good home, and she just wishes she knew somebody who would take them. I thought of you and wondered if you would be interested."

Sandi's legs turned to jelly as she groped for a chair.

"Twin boys?" she said faintly.

"Yes," Esther said. "They are two years old."

"I'd love to have them!" Sandi almost whooped with joy. Her heart skipped a beat, then raced with excitement. "And I know Philip will want them too!"

"How soon could you come to see them?" Esther asked.

"Let me call Philip at work and ask him," Sandi said. "I'll call you right back."

Philip was as excited as Sandi, but thinking more logically, he saw it was impractical to drop everything right then and run after the boys.

"The ordination is on Sunday, Sandi," he reminded her gently. "We can't go until that is over."

"Oh! I'm so excited, I forgot," Sandi laughed at

herself. "I guess you're right. But can we go right afterwards?"

"Monday morning," Philip promised.

Calls flew back and forth between all the women involved as arrangements were made for Philip and Sandi to meet the boys and their mother on Monday. Between the ordination and the possibility of getting twin boys, Sandi was so excited she could barely function.

"I can't believe God would call you to the ministry and give us children all in one whack," Sandi told Philip. "I think it's going to be either one or the other, but not both."

"I'm glad we can let it all in His hands," Philip said.

"So am I," Sandi agreed. But somehow, she was sure God was not going to do both things at once. If the choice were left to her, she knew what she would choose.

If it's going to be one or the other, let it be the children, God, she prayed. *Let it be the children.*

It meant so much to both Philip and Sandi to have Philip's mother attend the solemn ordination service. Tension mounted throughout the service, culminating when the two men sharing the lot each took a book from the table in front of the pulpit. They resumed their seats and waited for the bishop to see which book contained the slip of paper revealing the Lord's choice.

"The lot has been found in the book of Jonathan

Yoder," the bishop announced. Then he proceeded with the ordination of the new minister for the small congregation.

We're going to get the boys! Sandi's heart sang. *I knew God wouldn't do both things at once. He's going to give us the boys.* It was all she could do not to tell anyone the good news, but Philip and she had agreed to keep it to themselves until they were sure, just in case the mother changed her mind.

Taking Mom Hanson with them, Philip and Sandi left that evening and went to Philip's parents' home for the night. Esther had planned to meet them there the next day, bringing the boys with her.

Monday morning brought disappointment. "I'm sorry," Esther apologized, "but I can't find the mother or the boys. I'll keep trying and let you know as soon as I find them."

Sandi's heart sank. *Is this a wild goose chase?* she wondered. *Are my hopes about to be dashed again? Why does life keep doing this to me?*

"I found the boys at a baby sitter," Esther finally reported late in the day. "I'll bring them over tomorrow morning."

Sandi was ecstatic. Her hopes again rose to the sky. When Esther brought the twin boys to the door the next morning, it was love at first sight. One look at the obviously neglected and abused little boys was all it took for Sandi to understand just how they felt and what they needed. How well she knew the feeling behind the love-starved and fearful looks on their faces!

"This is Matthew and this is Marcus," Esther said, pointing to each in turn. "I'll leave you alone with them now. You can bring them to Elbys in about an hour, and I'll meet you there with their mother."

"Isn't it wonderful there are two of them?" Sandi exclaimed as she and Philip each picked up a boy. "Neither of us needs to have an empty lap."

The hour flew by as the prospective parents and grandparents got acquainted with the boys. At Elbys Philip and Sandi met Esther and the twins' mother who asked the prospective parents a few questions about how they intended to raise the boys.

"Are you ready to go to a lawyer?" the mother asked.

Startled, Philip and Sandi looked at each other. "Now?" they asked in unison.

"Yes," the mother said. "Esther has made arrangements with a lawyer in town, if you are ready to sign papers."

"Well . . ." Philip looked at Sandi questioningly. She nodded her head vigorously. "Yes!" he finished.

"I can't believe how fast this is happening," Sandi marveled as they drove to the lawyer's office. "I didn't expect to take them home today."

"At least you won't have to be in suspense anymore," Philip grinned.

The lawyer produced the two-year guardianship papers the mother requested, and also provided the initial paperwork to begin adoption proceedings. Concerned that they might be moving too fast, he cautioned everyone to be sure this is what they wanted to do before they signed.

When all the signatures were in their proper places, Sandi hugged the boys' mother.

"Thank you for having the courage to provide for these precious boys," Sandi said with teary eyes. "We will take good care of them, I promise."

"Send me pictures sometimes, so I'll know what they look like," the mother said.

"I'll do that," Sandi promised.

Philip shook hands with the mother and thanked her. Then Philip and Sandi loaded their precious cargo into the car and headed home. The boys whimpered at being taken away by these strangers.

"Poor dears, they only met us barely two hours ago," Sandi sympathized.

Soon she had them interested in their new surroundings, and their tears were forgotten.

Not having been prepared to bring the boys home that day, Philip and Sandi stopped for diapers and other necessities on the way home.

"Look at them," Sandi whispered as she peeked in the bedroom door that night. Two freshly-scrubbed, sweet-smelling little boys clad in new pajamas lay cuddled together in peaceful sleep. "I can't believe it. WE have twin boys!"

"You asked God for a baby," Philip reminded her. "And He gave us two. He opened the windows of heaven and poured out a blessing on us."

"I can't wait to see what people will say tomorrow night at prayer meeting," Sandi giggled. "This is so exciting. It's like when I met you. I seem to wait and wait for my prayers to be answered, and then, when God grants my requests, He works so fast I can hardly keep up with Him."

"We serve a wonderful God," Philip said reverently. "Let's pray now before we go to bed and thank Him for all His marvelous works in our lives."

"And ask Him to give us the wisdom and strength we need to raise Matthew and Marcus for Him," Sandi added seriously. "They are a great gift, but also a great responsibility."

As the brand new parents dropped to their knees, they poured out their hearts to the One on whom their faith was anchored. He had graciously granted their request and flooded their hearts with joy.

Chapter 34

Adjusting to life with two little boys in the house was both a challenge and an adventure for Philip and Sandi. Lacking both love and training, Matthew and Marcus required constant attention and supervision. Gradually, they came to understand and accept what was expected of them. Their patient, loving environment brought a stability and security into their lives unknown before. There were days when Sandi felt she and Philip had made no progress in the training department, but those days were more than offset by the boundless joy the boys added to their home.

Finalizing the adoption of Matthew and Marcus took two years of legal work. But when everything was completed at last and the boys were officially Hansons, Sandi felt like shouting the news from the housetops. At last, any fears of having them taken from her were laid to rest. They were hers to keep and love for the rest of their lives.

Recognizing the value of a plural ministry, the church at Rest Haven decided to ordain a second minister to serve with Brother Jonathan Yoder and help with the work of the church. Votes were taken late in November, and the congregation waited expectantly for Bishop Eli Glick to return and announce the results.

"Two brethren have been called to share the lot for minister," the bishop announced. "They are Brother Ronald Peachy and Brother Philip Hanson."

Oh no! Not again! Sandi thought. She well remembered the stress and anxiety of being in the lot before and did not look forward to going through it again.

"I really don't think it will be me," Philip confided when they were alone at home. "I know Mom always dreamed of my being in the ministry, and I felt for a long time I should preach. But I think if God wanted me to be ordained it would have happened the first time I was in the lot. God probably has plans for me other than preaching."

Philip and Sandi found the time between the vote taking and the ordination to be much less stressful than it had been the first time. They were at peace in their confidence that Ronald would be ordained.

The solemn ordination service, on December 5, 1994, followed the usual pattern of worship and reverent waiting upon God. Philip and Sandi sat on the front bench with Ronald and his wife. Both of Philip's parents attended the service this time.

Brother Elvin Miller preached the ordination message. Lack of anxiety about the ordination allowed Philip and Sandi to concentrate on the message. Their hearts were stirred anew with the claims of Christ upon their lives and their need to follow His call to them, regardless of His call to others.

The books were placed side-by-side in an upright position on the table in front of the pulpit. Bishop Eli Glick led in prayer, asking God to reveal His choice and then took his seat.

Softly the congregation began to sing, "Fully surrendered, Lord divine." Being older, Philip went forward first to choose a book.

"Where Thou leadest me, I will follow Thee," the congregation sang as Philip's hand closed on a book.

Sandi felt a sudden stab of panic rise within her. *It just MIGHT be him after all,* she realized with a start. Her heart raced, and her hands were suddenly clammy.

Ronald stood, took the remaining book, and returned to his seat.

When the song ended, the bishop came down from behind the pulpit, stood in front of Philip, and extended his hand for the book. With his head bowed, Philip handed it to him. Opening the cover, Brother Eli took out the slip of paper and held it aloft for the congregation to see.

"The lot has fallen upon Philip Hanson,"

Brother Eli announced.

With an almost audible sigh, the congregation relaxed as the tension eased. A rush of tears sprang to Philip's and Sandi's eyes with the knowledge of God's call and the weight of their new responsibility.

"My dear brother," Eli began the ordination ceremony, "the Lord has called you to be a minister of the Gospel of Jesus Christ. You may rise to answer several questions."

Philip, with Sandi by his side, rose and stood before the bishop. Brother Eli asked Philip three questions concerning his willingness to accept the ministry, his commitment to faithfully preach all the Word of God, and his willingness to lead the congregation according to the Gospel and in harmony with the other leaders.

After Philip answered "Yes" to all three questions, the bishop asked Sandi whether she was willing to support her husband and make any necessary sacrifices to help him fulfill his calling and responsibilities in the ministry.

"I am," Sandi answered quietly.

As Philip and Sandi knelt together, Brother Eli and a visiting bishop laid their hands upon Philip's head.

"Upon this confession and upon these promises that you have now made before God and these witnesses," Brother Eli began, "I herewith in the name of Jesus Christ and His church, charge and

242

ordain you to go and preach the Gospel in its purity; to warn the sinners, to admonish the unconverted to repent, to teach, instruct, comfort, and encourage the believers. Be instant in season and out of season, reprove, rebuke, and exhort with all longsuffering and doctrine. Do the work of an evangelist, and make full proof of your ministry. Likewise, take heed unto yourself; walk circumspectly, study the Word, meditate upon its precious precepts, pray without ceasing, and in all things seek to be a faithful laborer in the vineyard of the Lord. Continue in these things, for in so doing you shall save yourself and those that hear you. Amen."

The visiting bishop led in prayer, asking God to bless and guide Philip in his new responsibilities. He also invoked God's blessing upon Sandi for grace and strength to be a faithful, supportive wife.

When the prayer ended, Philip and Sandi rose to their feet. The officiating bishops greeted Philip with a holy kiss, giving him and Sandi both a few words of encouragement and the assurance of their prayers.

"I challenge you as a congregation to accept the calling of God for Brother Philip to be your minister," Brother Eli said as Philip and Sandi sat down. He urged those present to support Philip as he assumed the new responsibility of leading the congregation and preaching the Gospel.

A song of dedication and commitment was sung to close the service. With their throats choked with emotion, neither Philip nor Sandi was able to sing. But their hearts followed and sincerely repeated the words of the song.

Sandi was confident of Philip's ability to preach but felt unworthy of being a minister's wife. She could not help looking back to where she had come from and marvel at the mighty work of the Lord that had brought her step-by-step to this place. Although they had now been charged with an awesome responsibility, she knew the God who had met every need of their lives thus far, was also able to meet every need of the future. Surely He would not fail them.

Chapter 35

"I've been thinking," Philip said slowly, then paused before going on. "It's almost a year now since I've been ordained. The forty-five-minute drive to church is a real handicap. What would you think of moving closer?"

Sandi hesitated. She had thought of moving closer to the church, but had not mentioned it. The thought of leaving the little house where they had found so much happiness brought a keen sense of loss. Tumble-down though it was, this house was the only one they had ever owned. After so many years, it held many precious memories.

"I'm not excited about moving again," she said wistfully, looking slowly around her cozy kitchen with its wood-burning stove. "But I've been thinking about it myself, and I know it would be so much more convenient. Besides, the boys will need to start school next year. I'm not eager to move, but I'm willing, if we can find a suitable place we can afford."

"In a way, moving closer to the church will be more like going home than moving away from it,"

Philip observed. "Besides, a home is not a house, but the people in it."

"You're right," Sandi agreed. "Wherever you and the boys are, that is home to me."

Eventually the search for a house near Collings proved successful. The small peach and apple orchard that came with the place was a delightful bonus. When Sandi for the last time closed the door of the old house, now empty and stripped of its homey appeal, a wave of melancholy engulfed her. Anticipation of the house and community waiting for them, however, made leaving easier.

The disorganization involved in moving was only temporary. Within a week the house was in order, and their home resumed its normal routine.

"That was David Troyer from Indiana," Philip answered Sandi's questioning look as he turned from the phone. "He asked whether I would be the speaker at his church's weekend meetings. I said I'd pray about it and get back to him in a day or two."

"When is it?" Sandi wondered.

"The second weekend in September," Philip answered, flipping the calendar pages to that month. "Do you know any reason why it wouldn't suit to go?"

"No," Sandi said thoughtfully, looking at the dates Philip was pointing to. "What topic are they asking you to speak on?"

"The theme is 'Godly Wisdom,'" Philip said,

reading from his hurriedly scribbled notes. "It is divided into three messages: 'Wisdom for Spiritual Living,' 'Wisdom for Emotional Life,' and 'Wisdom for Practical Living.'"

"Sounds interesting," Sandi commented. "If you feel the Lord wants you to accept this invitation, I see no reason why we can't go."

The invitation to preach in Indiana was not the first Philip had received since his ordination. Invitations to churches across the country were increasing as people learned to know him and appreciate his ministry. Feeling the Lord had called him to go, Philip accepted the invitation, and the Hanson family made the trip.

"Are you sure this is the right place?" Sandi asked anxiously as Philip drove in a tree-shaded lane toward a two-story house surrounded by professional landscaping.

"According to the directions, it has to be," Philip nodded.

"They must be rich people," Sandi decided. "I wasn't looking for anything quite like this."

As the Hansons made their way across the porch, the front door of the house opened. A plainly dressed older man, followed by his wife, stepped out to meet them.

"Come on in," Dan and Emma Schrock invited warmly after the initial greetings had been exchanged.

Glancing through the door, Sandi saw that the

inside matched the outside. Rich wood tones, thick carpeting, draperies, and artful wall decorations combined to create a pleasing, attractive atmosphere.

I hope the boys know how to behave, Sandi thought in alarm. *I'll be mortified if they break something.*

"Have a seat," Emma invited. "Supper will be ready soon. I have just a few things to finish."

"Is there something I can do?" Sandi asked, following Emma to the kitchen.

"You may slice the bread," Emma graciously accepted Sandi's offer.

The two women began getting acquainted as they worked. Sandi soon realized her first impression, based on the fine appearance of the home, had been mistaken.

Emma is as down-to-earth as any of the women at home, Sandi thought as she poured water into the blue goblets matching the blue pattern in the fine china.

Moments after the blessing on the meal, Marcus accidentally spilled the water from his goblet.

"Oh, Marcus!" Sandi cried, as a stream of water spread rapidly across the tablecloth.

"No problem," Emma assured her, grabbing a tea towel and sopping up the spill.

"This table has seen lots of spills," Dan said with a comforting laugh. "When our children were at home we could hardly eat a meal without some-

248

one spilling their water."

"Yes," Emma laughed in agreement, "it was so bad, I used terry tablecloths for just that reason."

"Sounds like a good idea," Sandi smiled, making a mental note. "Thanks for the tip!"

The gracious way their host and hostess responded to the minor disaster set the entire Hanson family at ease. They relaxed and enjoyed the fellowship during the rest of the meal.

The congregation in Indiana was much larger than the one at Rest Haven. There were also obvious differences in what were acceptable church standards. But faith in Christ was a common bond on which they could build relationships. New acquaintances were made and friendships were formed between sessions. Before it seemed possible, the weekend was history, and it was time to make the long trip back to Oklahoma.

"I've sure learned a lot since we came into the Mennonite church," Sandi broke the silence as the miles of Interstate 70 slipped rapidly behind them.

"In what way?" Philip questioned, unsure where her thoughts had been.

"Well," Sandi hesitated, glancing at the sleeping boys on the back seat. "When we first went looking for Mennonites, all we knew was what we had read in books. We read there were different types of Mennonites, but I didn't realize how much variation there is. All we knew were the ones we met at Rest Haven and in our area. I guess I thought

249

all Mennonites were like them, even though I had read otherwise. The more we are getting into different areas, the more I see how little I knew. It really can be confusing."

"I know what you mean," Philip agreed. "I thought being 'plain' meant a simple lifestyle of separation from the world in every area. Then we see people who dress themselves simply, but dress up their homes. What is considered conservative in one area is considered liberal in another. And yet, those in each group feel they are practicing nonconformity to the world."

"I'm glad we didn't see all these things before our beliefs were settled," Sandi said. "If we had been exposed to all the differences earlier, I'm afraid I might have become so confused that I would have given up in despair."

"God has been faithful in leading us all the way," Philip declared. "Back in the beginning we were sort of like hothouse plants in a sheltered environment until our roots were deep enough to support us.

"Not having grown up in Mennonite homes gives us a somewhat different perspective on some things," he went on. "We have had to think through our own convictions and decide what is right and wrong on each issue, while some Mennonites take what is handed to them without much thought. Then, when new trends come along, they may accept those things before considering all the implications. There is no perfect church anywhere, and Mennonites struggle with the same temptations Christians face everywhere."

"How right you are!" Sandi exclaimed. "We see the church more realistically now than we did when we became members. There are both strengths and weaknesses. I'll admit, it was disappointing to discover everything is not as ideal as I first thought. Deciding who is right and who is wrong on every detailed application of Biblical principles is not the most important thing. To me, the most important thing is to see that I am doing what God tells me to do, regardless what others think, say, or do."

"You're right," Philip agreed. "Some of the standards we have set for our family may not be what others have decided on for their family. But we are following the Lord. The choices we make in life are based on what we believe is His will for us and not on what others do."

"When we became members, the bishop encouraged us to maintain our simple lifestyle and not to feel pressured to conform to any group inside the church," Sandi said. "I didn't know then what he meant, but I do now. He understood the peer pressure inside the church as well as outside of it. I want to remember, it was when Peter took his eyes off the Lord and looked at his surroundings that he sank in the water. If we keep focused on Christ, instead of comparing ourselves with others, He

will surely help us through all the ups and downs
of life."

Chapter 36

"We've been so busy in the orchard that I haven't had time to can any peaches," Sandi remarked over breakfast as the peach harvest came to a close. "I have some seconds set back, and if I don't get at them soon, they'll spoil. But I just don't see how I'll get them done."

"Maybe you could get a girl to come help you," Philip suggested.

"Maybe," Sandi said thoughtfully. "I wonder if Almeta could spare Rosy for a day. Or maybe Janice could come. I'll see if I can find somebody," she said as she reached for the phone.

"The boys can go to the orchard with me," Philip said.

"Fine," Sandi agreed as she dialed.

Almeta willingly agreed to let her seventeen-year-old daughter help Sandi. Rosy arrived later in the morning, and despite their age difference the two women visited companionably as they cut and peeled peaches.

"It goes so much faster with two people peeling,"

Sandi said, looking with satisfaction at the row of filled jars waiting to go into the canner.

"Mom says . . ." Rosy began, but left the sentence unfinished as the phone rang and Sandi jumped up to answer it.

Although she tried not to listen, Rosy could not help overhearing part of the conversation. Sandi was talking to someone Rosy did not know.

"That was my mother," Sandi explained when she returned to Rosy and the peaches.

"Oh," Rosy said hesitantly, not knowing what else to say.

"Mama calls me more often than she used to, which I'm glad for," Sandi said.

Rosy said nothing.

"You don't know how good you have it, being born into a Christian home," Sandi said fervently, voicing her thoughts that had filled the silence between them. "Mama has been married and divorced six times. Since her last divorce, she has been doing better. She doesn't bother with men anymore, has stopped drinking, and is trying to live right. My sisters both divorced their first husbands and are remarried. They both have children. My little brother Jimmy became a Christian when he was sixteen. I try to encourage him all I can to be faithful to the Lord and live for Him. I hope and pray he will be spared the heartaches of a sinful life."

Rosy listened sympathetically as Sandi went on,

sharing the story of her life. They laughed and cried together as Sandi told the joys and sorrows of her childhood.

"I used to try to make everything right in my family," Sandi confided as she ended her story. "I realize now there is not much I can do. God is the only One who can make everything right. Each person is responsible to respond when God calls. Still, after all this time, I find myself hoping that all my family will come to know the Lord and find real joy and fulfillment in living. I will never stop praying for them, for as long as there is life, there is hope."

"I wish I could help Mennonite young people see all the advantages and blessings they have," Sandi said wistfully after a brief silence. "Philip and I looked so long and hard to find what we have now. It hurts me to see Christian young people, taught the Bible since they were born, throw it away and go out into the world looking for fun and happiness. Others flirt with the world for a few cheap thrills and don't see where it could take them. I've been there, and believe me, the world has nothing to offer. I wish I could tell young people that."

"You ought to write a book and tell the story of your life," Rosy said enthusiastically.

"Oh, I couldn't do that," Sandi protested.

"Why not?" Rosy persisted. "If people would read your life's story, they could see the difference Christ makes. People you'll never be able to meet could read it and be encouraged to be faithful to the Lord. If even one person would turn to Christ as a result, it would be worth it."

"But I'm not a writer," Sandi objected. "I didn't have a very good education. I could tell you my story, but putting it on paper would be altogether different. I can't express my thoughts on paper."

"Then ask the Lord to lead you to someone who will do it for you," Rosy encouraged.

"I'll think about it," Sandi agreed. "If the Lord wants me to tell my story, He'll provide a way."

"I'll pray about it too," Rosy promised as she tightened the lid on the last jar of peaches.

"Oh, my!" Sandi exclaimed with a startled glance at the clock. "Philip and the boys will be in for dinner any minute. I'm surprised they haven't come in already. At this hour, it will have to be soup and sandwiches!"

The remaining weeks of summer flew by. Fall brought with it changes in scenery and schedule as school days began.

"My throat hurts," Matthew complained one morning as he entered the kitchen.

"Open your mouth and let me see," Sandi said, observing his flushed cheeks and droopy-looking eyes.

Just as she had expected, two red, swollen tonsils bulged out on the sides of his throat. The thermometer revealed a temperature of 100.

"You just lie down on the sofa," Sandi

instructed. "I'll make some tea and give you some medicine for your fever."

In spite of Sandi's care, Matthew's condition worsened as the day wore on. After a restless night, his temperature had risen to 103. Sandi took him to the doctor in the morning and received a bottle of antibiotics to fight off the strep infection in his throat.

"Now open wide," Sandi said, pouring out a spoonful of medicine when they returned home. "This will taste good and make you feel much better."

Matthew obediently opened his mouth and swallowed the medicine. "Hold me, Mama," he begged.

"Of course I'll hold you, Sweetheart," Sandi murmured.

Carrying him to the rocking chair, she sat down and held him close to her heart. He snuggled against her as she began rocking slowly back and forth, humming "Blessed Assurance." Relaxed and contented, his eyes closed and he fell asleep, secure in his mother's love and care. Reluctant to put him down, Sandi continued to hold and rock him. She looked down at his still-flushed face.

"Hold me, Mama," he had said. The echo of those words brought back the memory of a miserably sick little girl standing at the head of a stairway, crying down to her mother for comfort. She remembered how unwanted she had felt when

Mama refused to hold her. She could still feel the dreadful loneliness and rejection, suffering alone upstairs as her mother partied.

Tears spilled down Sandi's cheeks as she looked at the dear face of the sleeping boy in her arms, and compared herself to him. God had answered her prayers and delivered her from the violent, abusive home and lifestyle in which she grew up. Being freed from that bondage now enabled her to help rescue these two precious boys from the same kind of life. What a privilege it was to point them to the Lord at this young age!

It's so common to hear people blame their problems on their parents and dysfunctional homes, Sandi thought as she got up and took Matthew to his bed. *My life is living proof that no one is doomed to repeat the failures and sinful lifestyle of his parents. God can change things. Anyone who thinks his situation is hopeless can find in God an anchor of hope. Nothing is too hard for the Lord.*

Christian Light Publications, Inc., is a non-profit conservative Mennonite publishing company providing Christ-centered, Biblical literature in a variety of forms including Gospel tracts, books, Sunday school materials, summer Bible school materials, and a full curriculum for Christian day schools and homeschools.

For more information at no obligation or for spiritual help, please write to us at:

Christian Light Publications, Inc.
P. O. Box 1212
Harrisonburg, VA 22801-1212